I'm Still SINGING

Bishop Dr. Barbara Ward Farmer

AuthorHouse™
1663 Liberty Drive
Bloomington, IN 47403
www.authorhouse.com
Phone: 1-800-839-8640

© 2014 Bishop Dr. Barbara Ward Farmer. All rights reserved.

Front cover image Edward Ward lll

No part of this book may be reproduced, stored in a retrieval system, or transmitted by any means without the written permission of the author.

Published by AuthorHouse 8/18/2014

ISBN: 978-1-4969-3344-7 (sc)
ISBN: 978-1-4969-3343-0 (hc)
ISBN: 978-1-4969-3342-3 (e)

Library of Congress Control Number: 2014914339

Any people depicted in stock imagery provided by Thinkstock are models, and such images are being used for illustrative purposes only. Certain stock imagery © Thinkstock.

This book is printed on acid-free paper.

Because of the dynamic nature of the Internet, any web addresses or links contained in this book may have changed since publication and may no longer be valid. The views expressed in this work are solely those of the author and do not necessarily reflect the views of the publisher, and the publisher hereby disclaims any responsibility for them.

Contents

Dedication vii
Acknowledgement ix
Foreword xiii
Chapter 1   "The Sound of Music" 1
Chapter 2   "My Parents" 7
Chapter 3   "My Siblings" 13
Chapter 4   "My Children" 19
Chapter 5   "Musical Influences" 25
Chapter 6   "Why Am I Different?" 33
Chapter 7   'The Impact of Salvation' 37
Chapter 8   "New Journey, New Experiences" 51
Chapter 9   "The Wagner Alumni Choir" 57
Chapter 10 "The National CLG Music Conference" 63
Chapter 11 "From Spiritual Ministry to Spiritual Leader" .. 67
Chapter 12 "International Traveler" 77
Chapter 13 "I'm Still Singing!" 81
Chapter 14 "Something To Sing About: A Chronological Scope of My Lifetime Achievements" 85
Epilogue 93

Dedication

To my Mom, Bishop and Overseer – *Bishop Lillian Ward*, and **to my Dad**, *the late Elder Edward Ward, Sr.,* who birthed me into what I am today and how I see God in Jesus Christ and His Church.

To my husband, Larry, who has not only been my trumpet player, but my lover, friend, confidant, encourager, father to our children, and a true yet quiet man of God. *"I'm really glad I married you."*

To my children: *Larita, Benita, Sharita Joy, and Larry Jr.,* for your specialty in just being good and special kids. *"You and your dad have kept me singing and now you're singing your own songs!"*

To my five brothers and sisters: *Edward Jr.* (June Bug), *Brenda* (no joke!), *Elder Lorraine* (the Preacher Lady but also 'Racket Squad'), *Elder Carole* (Merry the Better), and *Byron* (a musical genius – 'never could've made it without you!). *"Mommy taught us to be close. We can't help ourselves!"*...

Thanks to everyone who has ever seeded music into my life in public school – *Mrs. Blackwell, Mr. Nelson, Mr. Colon, Mrs. Clark* (Ranges Temple Trio fame), *Mr. Yeats,* and *Dr. Alifaris.* **And, from my college years** – *Ms. Lois Williams, from West Chester State College, now West Chester State University.*

To my West Chester and Wagner Alumni and Friends Choirs: *"I shall never forget our good times while making good music."*

To my Faith Tabernacle Church Family – *"Thank you for being my most devoted support down through the years."*

To the singers, musicians, writers and arrangers everywhere who've maintained the Word of God through song – *"You have inspired and energized me."*

Very Special Thanks to my Church of The Living God (CLG) mentors who encouraged and blessed me to sing and perform. The late Bishop L.C. Williams of Pennsgrove, NJ, my first pastor and role model as a purveyor of excellence in all that we do, in all facets of ministry as a woman at home *and* in the church. Her daughter - my godmother, *Rev. Garnita Selby,* also a purveyor of excellence; the *late Professor Edward G. Robinson* from Detroit, MI., *Brothers Jerry and Benjamin Drone* from Akron, Oh., and my special co-worker in the music vineyard whom I will always cherish – *Bishop Roger Hairston* from Columbus, Oh. From the CLG Body in which I grew up, a plethora of mentors supported me - from Rhode Island to Florida, New Jersey to Wisconsin, Illinois to Mississippi, Liberia to Ghana, and from Jamaica to Trinidad. All of them blessed me, and to them all I extend a heartfelt *"Thank you!"*

To the families of now deceased 'piano men' who played for me when I was a child: *Bernard A. Chandler, Jimmy Smith, and Brother Forrest,* all from Philadelphia, PA., where I first started singing. And, for the unnamed *'piano men'* of the 1950's who from the crowd volunteered to play for me spontaneously and without pay while answering the call, "Is there a pianist in the house?"

Acknowledgement

It is a well-known fact that places such as Detroit, MI, Nashville, TN, and Chicago, IL, breed good singers, choirs, musicians, and writers. However, it should be noted that in the gospel world, Philadelphia and its surrounding areas must be added to this list.

From my earliest memories, the 'Philadelphia Sound' was conceived in Gospel before the 'secular' Philadelphia Sound was conceived and popularized. Before Dee Dee Sharpe, Chubby Checker, Frankie Avalon and Fabian, there was Madame Bumpus, the Ward Singers, Rudolph Lewis, the Davis Singers, the Stars of Faith, the Imperials, The Savettes, the Victory Choral Ensemble, the Philadelphia Mass Choir, Sandra Peyton, Ernest Davis, the Troubadours, Morris Scott, the Newberry Singers, and Irvin Brockington and the Brockington Ensemble. Later, there was Ernest Davis and the Wilmington Chester Mass Choir, Dawkins New Sound, Gloria Neal and the Ladies of Song, Isaac Douglas, and New Jersey's Freddie Washington and the Washington Family Ministry, the Gabriel Hardeman Delegation, and numerous quartets and women's groups emerged from the Philadelphia/New Jersey/New York Tri-State area.

I thank God for the many church choirs in the Philadelphia area that groomed and supported their music ministry and produced choirs that exalted the magnificent name of Christ. Choirs from the various Baptist, Methodist, Apostolic and Holiness churches made recordings while supporting their pastors with excellence and dedication for many years. Some of these churches that I can recall were: Second Pilgrim, Cornerstone Baptist, B.M Oakley Fellowship, the Highway Churches of Christ, Christian Tabernacle, Rock of Ages (Camden, NJ), and the acclaimed Joy Night Choirs, New Jersey/Pennsylvania Fellowship Choirs, and the United Holy Church of America Choirs, which consisted of members from various choirs from different denominations.

Philadelphia's musicians are so plentiful that to mention some and not others would be a real disservice to the gospel music ministry. But, I want to acknowledge the musicians and directors who served with me throughout my ministry: Bernard Chandler, Jimmy Smith, and Brother Forest were my first piano players as a child soloist. Rev. Steven Ford, Bishop Andrew (Andy) Ford, Rev. Leon Frison, Rev. 'Ting' Burke, Rev. Garfield, Williams, Bishop Howard (Buddy) Crosby, David Bell, and Calvin Carr were instrumental on the Sweet Rain Record label. Elder Hubert Powell of Hartford, CT gave us two fantastic songs on Wagner's second album.

If I was considered to be the 'musical mother' to some of the young and gifted musicians who evolved and blessed me along the way, I'd extend special thanks to my 'musician children' – Pastor Ronald King, Sr., principal writer of Wagner Alumni songs that are still sung today. To my baby brother, Byron Ward, who arranged most of Wagner's songs. To our guitar players: Rev. David Burno, lead guitar; Rev. Jared Crawford, bass. To our drummers: Rev. Robert 'Lavel' Johnson, Elder Walter Lewis, and Mark Crawford. To our keyboard/organists: Rev. John

Parker, Jr., Rev. Rodney Green, Jimmy Boisseau, and Lawrence Farmer, Jr. To Elder John 'Juggles'

Thompson, the Blackson Brothers – Gene and Brian, Vernon Dykes, and Warren Harding, who faithfully comprised our horn section. Pastor Ronald King, Lori Toland, Leonard Kennedy and Bishop Joel Adams assisted me in the area of directing – they were the best. Thanks be to God for His generosity in assigning talents and gifts. To that end, Barbara Ward Farmer was not the only lead singer on the Wagner albums, for Overseer Wendell Miller and Elder Carole Ellerbe (my sister), sang lead on all of Wagner's projects. Additionally, Pastor Michelle Ford Johnson, Charlene Connelly, Charmaine Ford, the late Juanita Burno, Eddie Davis, and my friend Margaret Estelle from Hartford, CT., led songs beautifully on some of our projects. Special mention is necessary to my musical sons who blessed me with their talents during the Wagner days: Minister Teddy Johnson of Las Vegas, Nevada, and Curtis Andrews Jr., of Harrisburg, PA., and Jamar Jones, formerly of Phila., PA, now serving at the Potter's House and living in Dallas, TX.

The choirs or personalities that most affected me in my outlook regarding teaching, training, or performing, is the 'church sound' on wax-form are: the Institutional Radio choirs of the 60's and 70's, the Thompson Community Choir from Chicago, for their unique sound (loved those tenors!); the Hawkins Singers for their style, flair and lyrics; and Pastor Shirley Caesar, who I had the honor of personally meeting at our church in Penns Grove, NJ., in the late 60's. I have never forgotten her zeal and honesty about how to minister. Finally, I believe my directing ability is a combination of many people from school days and various conferences that I observed and participated in. But it was the late Dr. Mattie Moss Clark from Detroit, MI., who impressed me to direct commanding what you want and you'll get what you command. This Mighty Woman of God taught me by demonstration that "when the ingredient of good voices, good breathing, and good memory of words are mixed together and directed toward a goal, you will achieve what you want – a good sound that ministers." ...And God is glorified!!!

Foreword

The beauty of singing and making music is that it is a shared experience. Thus, it takes a special person who relishes in sharing with others the gift of music in whatever its' form, to do it effectively, tenaciously, and selflessly. The sharing that I refer to in this instance is not merely about 'performance,' but about a life of *ministry through music*: from singing, to playing, to teaching music in the classroom and the church, and most prominently through an exemplary Christian life that Divinely demonstrates how to live for Christ and minister music to others, when and wherever. Truly, this is using a gift to answer the call to perpetuate the Gospel in the entire world, just as Jesus commanded us all to do. ***"Go ye into all the world and spread the Good News of Jesus Christ, teaching all nations." Matthew 28:19-20.***

As you will experience in reading the pages of this book, Bishop Barbara Ward Farmer personifies the statements above. She exemplifies the declarative song of praise, "I Just Couldn't Keep It to Myself," which she modernized with the Wagner Alumni Choir when they sang, "You'd Better Tell Somebody!" And all of her life, from the time that she first accepted Christ at the tender age of 7 yrs. old, her desire and drive have been to bless the LORD with the gift He favored her with, and in doing so, she and her music have been a blessing to literally multitudes. For, one who started out as a little wide-eyed girl in South Philadelphia singing the Gospel of Jesus Christ by mimicking others, developed into an anointed young leader, teacher, mother, mentor, pastor, and bishop. Along the way, through her 'sharing,' she has 'prepared others to do the same.' For many leaders in the public, private and religious sectors attribute their relationship with Christ, their families, their ministries, and their overall successes to their association with this Mighty Woman of God. Others who met her later in life and did not know her as a young teacher-mentor, testify of being blessed by the influence her life has had on their own whether they met her as a sinner, saint, congregant, leader, pastor, bishop, musician or politician. This Mighty Woman of God exudes Godly Presence wherever she goes, and she is masterful in the art of conveying the Word of God through music. In fact, she has never used music in any other way.

As you read this book you will realize how her steps have truly been ordered by the LORD. She'll tell you that she's been bought with a price. She's not of her own and does not act on her own - this is apparent. We see it in her actions. Hear it in her music. Feel it in her presence. As we are moved by her, blessed by her, influenced by her – we are truly witnessing and experiencing the power of God in action. We are blessed to have this vessel of God who so willingly allows His Spirit, that of the Living God, to flow through her unto us to do His will. We are the benefactors of her obedience and God is glorified!!!

Of course, one might say that because she is my cousin I'm biased. No need to be because ANYONE who knows her will say the same, even if they've known for only a moment. I hope the readers of this book will feel the experience of her journey from birth to today and the *Ever Presence of God in her life every step of the way.* I hope you will also share the excitement that she felt as her story evolves, for I want you to know that the family shared in it at those times as well.

Bishop Farmer or 'Barbara Ann' as we call her, was a constant topic of conversation and source of excitement and pride for us with every musical accomplishment and invitation to appear with gospel artists that were the talk of the day.

Through it all, she's remained consistent – steadfastly focused on Jesus Christ. I'm sure that I speak for many when I say, "Thank you Bishop Farmer, for every song you've sung." Somebody's soul has been saved, healed, delivered, and encouraged because of it. From every melody and rhythm has come release, joy, redemption, and restoration. Somebody has had a life-changing experience of mind, soul, and yes, even of body because of you. And for many, that has only been the beginning. **For, you have stood the test of time – "You're Still Singing!"** And, because you still sing, many of us who you've blessed and taught to bless others, still sing too. Yours is the voice that we never grow tired of hearing. It is the voice of God and we are grateful for your obedience in conveying His word and power to us through music for six (6) decades. Your singing/preaching voice has borne much fruit that glorifies God, as is witnessed to in this book. So, thank you for your time, sacrifice, and obedience, Bishop. Prayerfully, you will always have something to sing about and never tire of sharing your song. Your work has undoubtedly added increase to the heavenly chorus. And, someday, we will sing together to the glory of God throughout eternity!!!

Love,
Dr. Shirley F. McDougald

Chapter One

"The Sound of Music"

Often, it is said that music is a universal language. For me, that means that music is understood in all seven continents of the world, in all of the thousands of capitals of the world, in all one hundred and ninety-three countries of the world, and in every hamlet and village of the earth. Although words are different from language to language and dialect to dialect, the universal connection that music has that connects us to it and leads us to like or dislike it is the 'sound.' According to *the Infoplease English Dictionary*, sound is:

1. The sensation produced by stimulation of the hearing organs by the vibrations transmitted through the air or other medium,
2. The particular auditory sound of music,
3. Any auditory effect – any audible vibrational disturbance; and
4. A noise, vocal utterance, musical tone or the like.

I am told that from an early age, I had an awareness of sounds and a sensitive ear to them all like *every day noises*: a baby's cry, a passing truck, a whispering willow, a barking dog, a clanking noise, a flying plane; *musical instruments*: i.e., a piano, organ, violin, flute, harmonica, harp, drums, cello, saxophone, trombone, trumpet, tambourine, guitar, bass guitar, and the piccolo. And, to the *volume of sound:* loud, soft, long, sustained, staccato, crescendos, decrescendos; and *sound pitch:* high, low, sharp, and flat. When I was growing up, all of these sounds were known to me simply as 'vibrations' that were foreign to my everyday common ear.

'Sounds of My Youth'

Most children respond to loud noises, sudden noises, and conversely, to sounds that calm them like the sound of a lullaby. Grade school sounds of 'Twinkle-Twinkle Little Star,' 'Bah-Bah Black Sheep Have You Any Wool,' and 'Row, Row, Row Your Boat,' were songs that I heard sung repeatedly as a child, and now the sound of these songs still have meaning even today. For me, these early *'sounds of music'* had a special meaning – I simply loved them all!!!

Another sound that had special meaning to me growing up in the 1950's was the patriotic songs like: 'This Is My Country!' 'My Country Tis Of Thee,' 'America the Beautiful,' and of course, Francis Scott Keys', 'Star Spangled Banner.' The 50's were the times of the Cold War coming out of the Second World War in Europe, and all the propaganda was geared toward love of country, love of family, and love of freedom. In the Wards' household in South Philadelphia, among the poor 'colored' or 'Negro' population (that's what we were called in the 1950's) sounds of school and church were all that we knew.

'The Early Church Sound'

As a child of the 50's, my mother took us to her father's church in Philadelphia on Grays Ferry Ave., across from an area called "The Roads." My maternal grandfather, Bishop Joseph Daniel McDougald was a man relatively short in stature, dark-skinned, hefty, and a fireball of a preacher who not only preached and taught hard, but I remember him playing what is now called the *"stride piano."* The sound of church for me at age 7 or 8 was that of an upright, out-of-tune piano (I know this now, but I didn't know it then), and a bass drum that was beaten with a stick with some kind of ball at the tip of it that was used for good emphasis in the service to bring on the praise! And then there was someone who played or beat a washboard with a spoon or a bent up wire hanger that ran the demons and devils right on out of you during a high service of deliverance.

While I remember my mother singing in what we at the time called the *"Devotional and Testimony"* portion of the worship experience, my Dad also displayed musical ability with the *'church sound'* that still resonates in me today. It was in the 50's that we heard the *'church sound'* in songs like: *'When We All Get To Heaven,' 'I'm A Soldier In The Army of The LORD,' 'In The Name of Jesus,' 'In The Morning When I Rise,' 'The Windows of Heaven,' 'You've Got To Move,' 'Bye and Bye,' 'Jesus, I'll Never Forget What You've Done For Me,' 'Oh, Oh, Oh, Oh, What's He's Done For Me,' 'At The Cross,' and 'I Know It Was The Blood.'* As I reflect on those times, I realize that the sound was repetitive yet energetically sung with power, emotion, and conviction. These were examples of the *'sounds of the church,'* which were to be sung *in* church, and *for* the church. Any other *'sound'* was considered for school, which was okay, but not the other sound, the *'secular sound'* which we heard in the streets, on the radio, or at a birthday party where 'worldly' or 'rock n roll' music might be played. These sounds were NOT okay. The Word of God tells us in Psalms 100 to *'make a joyful noise **unto the LORD**.'* That's the sound that the LORD wants to hear from His people.

"God Inspired Sounds"

The sounds of music that shaped my life were most definitely the sounds of my youth and the sounds of my early church experience. Looking back, I now know that much was instilled in me by my environment, which included my home with my mother and father, my siblings, and my grandfather's church – the Universal Bible Church of God, in Philadelphia. This was an appropriate name for his church and between the ages of 3 and 7 I believe, it was there that I became acquainted with or was introduced to the *'sound of God.'*

The only way that I can explain this sound is to explain what I believe what happened in the Garden of Eden. Adam and Eve were aware that they were special. They were the first to experience the *'sound of God.'* This sound is the way God is and it is the *'who'* of God. God, The Eternal, both before Genesis and after Revelations, does not ever have to be seen, but He is always heard. His way is heard; His *'who-ness'* is also heard. When God wants, He speaks. His voice makes a sound. What He says makes a sound that stimulates and moves the target of His affection to respond. In the Garden, God hovered or moved, which created a sound. Adam and Eve were familiar to the sound of God. They had no visual, just a sound – a sound of the invisible God whose sound was visible. His sound was heard and light was formed; so were the sky, seas, rivers, moon and stars. The *'sound of God,'* which is an expression of who He is, was heard when Adam sinned. How, you may ask? Let's look at Genesis 3:8-10: "And they heard the voice of the LORD walking in the garden in the cool of the day: and Adam and his wife hid themselves from the presence of the LORD God amongst the trees of the garden." And the LORD God called unto Adam, and said unto him, "Where art thou?" And he said, "I heard Thy voice in the garden, and was afraid because I was naked, and I hid myself."

I'm Still Singing

Now, my friends, when was the last time you've heard anyone's *voice* walking – anywhere? Well, the reason I believe Adam heard God's voice walking is because Adam had a relationship with God's sound, and He realized by the sound of His voice that God was not pleased. It is a known fact that each one of our senses affects the other senses when challenged. For example, what Adam heard (the sound of God's displeasure), affected his visual. He noticed that now he was naked (he was naked all along and it hadn't mattered before). God's sound changed when Adam and Eve sinned (everyone takes notice when one goes from *'piannisimo'* to *'forte,' 'soft'* to *'loud'* in a sound shift). Adam heard the *key change, the volume change, and the decrescendo* from his original state to the state of a fallen creation.

I believe that the sound of God has been heard throughout His creative works. Whenever God speaks – a transformation, a shift, and/or a reformation is inevitable to occur. And, the *'sound of God'* is always *God inspired.*

As a child, my parents introduced the sound of God to us in our family home. We were taught to reverence God, to respect Him, to love Him, and honor Him. Although I didn't have a relationship with God between ages 3-7, my mother taught me about God and who He is – The Omnipotent One, The Omnipresent One, The Great I Am. He was the Way to go to heaven. So, as a child, heaven was a place that I wanted to go to be with Jesus. That meant that we shouldn't say bad words, cuss, steal, kill, cheat, or fight. Thus, God's sound was heard in my life with the knowledge of right and wrong. This was a God inspired sound that would truly affect the next phase of my life.

Chapter Two

"My Parents"

It has been said that you are a product of your environment. Well, I don't know who first said it, but this statement is certainly true in my life as I think of how it began and unfolded over 63 years ago. And this truth is because of the lives of two people – my parents, Edward and Lillian Ward.

My father, Rev. Edward Ward, Sr., was born on May 8, 1918 in North Carolina, to Mary and Lincoln Ward. Although neither of his parents raised him, his children were a reflection of a large portion of his life. My father told us that he never really knew his father, and didn't get acquainted with his biological mother, Mary, until his young adult life. Daddy was raised by his maternal grandmother who according to his own words, was an almost "white looking woman who was stern and mean," and raised my dad to be isolated – repeatedly leaving him alone to play by himself which caused him to eventually become sort of a dreamer. He said that because of this environment of isolation, he would often dream of having a family that he could love and who in turn would love him. Thank God, Dad never revealed any abuse to us, which would explain why he was calm and quiet about dealing with situations in the house and later on in his life.

Because my dad was raised as a lone child, he was set in his ways. Fortunately, he later learned that he had four (4) other sisters and brothers who he eventually met in Philadelphia, Pennsylvania, years later. He could only finish the 8th grade, forced to work in the fields. Now, I believe that this action revealed two things about my dad's behavior later on in his life. I believe that although he merely completed 8th grade, Dad developed an independence and acquired a thirst for knowledge. He was resourcefully and aptly self-taught. As his thirst for knowledge grew, Dad established his own library of books that ranged from health or related issues to psychology and human behavior. I know because I would read some of those books and magazines that Daddy regularly ordered from the publishing houses. Daddy could have easily gotten what we now know as a GED (Graduate Equivalent Diploma), but there was no such thing available to him, for the GED was initiated in the 1940's for returning military to give them academic credentials that would enable them to gain access to civilian jobs and gain access to secondary education. It remained that way for many years before it was offered to the general public. Needless to say, Daddy did not qualify, however, he became an avid reader and learned man on his very own.

Daddy was always a truly hardworking man. His positive work ethic is the second thing that I believe my dad's early departure from school to work in the fields lead him to. He worked at the Campbell Soup Company in Camden, N.J., for over 30 years without missing a day of work! After he retired at 65 years of age, he kept on working at various cooking and cleaning jobs for over ten (10) years because Daddy believed in working. I don't think he particularly 'loved' to work, but I think he saw the 'need' to work to support himself and his family, a family that God would eventually expand to seven (7) people besides him. Thus, his family included a wife of 56 years, and six (6) children. There is so much more that I could say about this giant of a man and what he really meant to me, my Mom, and my sisters and brothers, and maybe that will be another book. For now, I would like to talk about how my musical talents can be traced back to both my paternal and maternal heritage and influence.

Upon reflection, I now realize that when I was a young girl growing up in South Philly (South Philadelphia), it was my maternal grandfather, the late Bishop Joseph Daniel McDougald - founder of the Universal Bible Church of God, who planted the seed in me as a child to understand and even appreciate music. Although a gifted '40's and '50's era, fire and brimstone, standing 'flat-footed' and telling the truth preacher and prognosticator of the Gospel, he was also a musician of sorts who dazzled his storefront congregation as he played the upright brown wooden mostly out-of-tune piano as a prelude to stepping into the pulpit and 'preaching until fire rained and the Glory of God fell!' What made him unique as a 'musician of sorts' was that he played, as my cousin Shirley recalls, the piano with two fingers in the key of C major. Now, this may not seem unusual for most people, but he played the same pattern arrangement for every song: basic left octave C notes first, with the right hand chorded with C-E four times; followed by F octave notes with the left hand, with the right hand with F-A two times; followed by the same pattern with C, then varying to G octave notes (left) with the right hand with G-B natural two times, and then back to C. Now, my grandfather played this same pattern for almost every song! Those of you who are familiar with the Pentecostal/Apostolic-type worship of his day are familiar with the devotional service type of songs that were sung such as, *'In the Morning When I Rise,' 'I'm A Soldier In The Army of The LORD,' 'I Know It Was The Blood,' 'The Holy Ghost and Fire Keeps On Falling, Thank God It Fell On Me,'* and countless others. My grandfather sang and led the devotional service with his beautiful, resonating baritone voice, and played the same chord pattern until a *'real'* musician showed up, usually my mother, who incidentally copied my grandfather to the 'T.'

As for my Dad, I remember seeing and hearing my father play the bass drum in church. His rhythm and sense of it was impeccable as I remember. You see, although my Dad had a quiet and humble manner about his character, he was a young minister who served God in the worship experience with passion and energy. He played the bass drum (I'm not sure what happened to the entire *drum trap set*, but back in the 50's that's what my dad played), and he played with such 'energy, zeal, and emotion' that eventually he'd cause the congregation to break out in a holy dance, right along with him.

I reiterate - Daddy was indeed a 'praiser.' My dear reader, understand what that phrase actually means to me. You see, my dad, with the consistent sound of the name of Jesus, would 'Shaback,' 'Yodah,' and dance as his expression of giving true thanks and gratitude to God flowed in the worship services. Dad was doing these types of praises before it became popular and even understandable in the late 80's and early 90's. Dad's isolative tendencies as an independent thinker of sorts, made him not really care what people said about how he passionately praised God or what they thought about how he gave glory and honor to the King of Kings, both in church and out of church. Now, please understand that I don't think anyone thought that he was 'kooky' or 'eccentric' even; rather, I sensed that everyone viewed my dad as a person who had a unique relationship with Jesus which was sincere, one who had his own personal touch and approach to praise, which made him quite unique.

Speaking of uniqueness, if you've ever met my mother, Lillian McDougald Ward, you would have to agree with me that there's one and only one her – now Overseer Lillian Ward. She is definitely a book all by herself. Raised by a mother whom she adored, and shaped in the preaching ministry by her preacher father, Mommy was destined to become the following things that affected how I saw the world both musically and socially:

---

1. Married my dad at age 22, ending his life of loneliness.
2. Gave birth to six (6) children who eventually would all be outstanding participants in the church and in society: Edward Ward, Jr. – Preacher, Mechanical Engineer and now Septa Specialist (Southeastern Pennsylvania Transportation); Brenda Stallworth Njoku, Ph.D – Business Mgr. and Educator, New Jersey School System; Elder Lorraine White – First Lady to Pastor Jesse White, Jr. of Hartford, CT., Elementary Education Principal in the Hartford, CT Public School System; Merry 'Carole' Ellerbe – Elder/Preacher/Teacher, Administrator/Principal in the New Jersey Public Schools System; and the youngest, Byron – Musician, Composer, Arranger, Producer, and decorated Philadelphia Police Officer, approaching 25 yrs. of service…(These are my siblings in birth order, with the exception of myself, the second born. My life is chronicled in this book so you'll read more about me later).
3. Displayed a definite ear for music. Formed a singing group of her own, comprised of neighborhood children. They were called the *'South Philadelphia Juniors'* (that's another book).
4. Showed early leadership skills as an organizer, developer, teacher of the Bible, and of character and respectability (to both men and women alike, but especially to young women).
5. Began preaching in her 30's in Penns Grove, New Jersey.
6. Began pastoring in a virtual *'church without walls'* in her neighborhood during the 1950's and 60's.

7. Began pastoring *'within walls'* in 1969 in Camden, NJ, where her husband, Edward Sr., served as her Assistant Pastor for over 25 years until his death.
8. Whenever the call of others was revealed, her Divine vision gave way to being an encourager to many in moving forward to preach, teach, or sing.
9. Finally, her life, demeanor, and character are personification of what faith is and what faith does. All of the above facts helped shape me both musically and spiritually. I am what I was to become because of my loving and powerful parental influences. This has and will forever impact my life – even into eternity. I will always be grateful to God for the parents He birthed me to, and to them for accepting their assignment. They have blessed me immeasurably and I aspire to emulate them in blessing my family and others.

Chapter Three

"My Siblings"

A Family of Levites

Down through the years, the Gospel world has been blessed by the rich music of the Hawkins Family, The Clark Sisters, The Winans, Andre Crouch and his sister Sandra; the Williams Brothers, and many, many, more. Traditional singers with family involvement were seen in large numbers in the 1930's, 1940's, and 1950's, and often they got their start by singing on the local or state church choir. Many church choirs back in the 1950's were usually, and in the 1960's were actually the Pastor and his children, who were the *first* of everything – first choir, usher, deacon, secretary, trustee, you name it – the Pastor or deacon's children were involved in everything.

My family was comprised of my father, mother, and six (6) children. We children didn't know that we were anointed or even what that meant. My father was the preacher in the family, and he was an Associate Minister at the church in which he found Christ. But, what was clear to my siblings and I was that we loved music! Quite early in our lives music surfaced as a smooth fit that required no assiduous effort for us to do. And, we were *always* singing! When it rained – we sang. When it was sunny – we sang. When we went on a day trip tightly packed in the family car – we sang. When we watched the

4-channel television set (the typical number of stations for TV sets in the '50's and '60's) – we would sing right along with the theme song for the show knowing every line of it right through to commercial – then we would sing that too! Oh yes, my siblings: Edward Ward Jr., Brenda Stallworth Njoku, Lorraine White, Merry Carole Ellerbe, and Byron Ward, Jr., were ordained by God to appreciate and love music. It was our destiny. We were anointed to express the *'sound of God'* in music.

Edward Ward, Jr. (June Bug)

A preacher born June 15, 1949, he is charismatic, athletic, and a worshipper. He married the former Anita Johnson of Wilmington, Delaware, to which three children were born: Edward (Eddie) Ward, III – a photographer and percussionist; Andre Ward, Sr. – a musical producer, entrepreneur, and guitarist; and Ashley Ward (the only daughter) – a gifted and anointed psalmist and worship leader bar none, and a gospel artist in her own right. She has blessed many with her anointed vocals in her home state of Delaware. My brother's offspring are a mirrored reflection of him and his gifts. For, both his children and grandchildren – Sydney, Lindsey, Edward IV (Eddie); Andre Jr., Amani, and Amber (Andre, Sr.); and even his daughters-in-law Lydia (Eddie) and Angie (Andre, Sr.) are both musically and athletically talented. Just like him.

Dr. Brenda Stallworth Njoku

The only Ph.D in the family. Born on June 26, 1952, she is a Special Education teacher. Although quick to tell you that she isn't a soloist, Brenda is a strong soprano and is comfortable singing background vocals. She has two (2) wonderful sons, Wayne and Cory. Both are musicians and Cory has additionally ventured into the area of arranging and producing. Brenda also has three (3) grandchildren – Isaiah, Armani, and Jaeden; and a daughter-in-law, Shawna (Cory).

Lorraine Ward White

Born on Independence Day, July 4th of 1954. She is the First Lady of the First Church of the Living God, in Hartford, Connecticut, where she serves with her husband, Pastor Jesse J. White, Jr. Lorraine is a stellar vocalist with an anointing that moves the congregation to their feet every time. Her anointing is palpable. She is an anointed vocalist *and* preacher. Pastor Jesse is himself a P-K's kid and grew up singing, playing the organ, and directing the choir under the pastoring of his father, Bishop Jesse White, Sr., during his administration at First Church. Both Lorraine and her husband have been involved in music in the churches in which they grew up (Faith Tabernacle and First Church, respectively), and in CLG churches statewide, and nationally, most, if not all of their lives. In fact, it was Lorraine who as a young adult initiated and directed the very first youth choir called the *'Voices of Faith'* at my parents' church, Faith Tabernacle CLG in Camden, NJ. She ministered in this musical capacity until she married and relocated to Hartford. She and her husband have (two) sons, Jesse III, and Joshua, who themselves are musicians. Jesse III (JJ) plays the guitar and drums, and Joshua (Josh) plays the organ and a 'mean' bass. Their wives, Walidah (JJ) and Stephanie (Josh) are both products of musical families and are gifted in their own right. Lorraine has three granddaughters, Savannah, Sara Belle, and Charli. Although all are quite young, we expect to hear from them musically in the near future.

Merry Carole Ellerbe

Born on December 10, 1958 with music in her bones! Like Lorraine and Brenda, she has a beautiful voice; and like Lorraine, she has the ability to teach others how to sing.

She became the Director of Faith Tabernacle's youth choir, *The Voices of Faith*, when her big sis Lorraine married and relocated to Hartford, CT. God, being the Preparer of what happens next, placed her in training for an eventuality – she would become an Educator and Administrator in the Camden NJ Public Schools. God has used her there to form the Woodrow Wilson Gospel Choir at Woodrow Wilson High School, and later she formed the Woodrow Wilson Alumni Choir. Although she does not play a musical instrument, Carol, as we call her, has an impeccable and keen musical ear, and is astute at teaching vocal parts to groups, choirs, and ensembles. She has recorded on three (3) albums as a soloist with the Wagner Alumni Choir, and has directed Mass Choirs at our home church Faith Tabernacle, CLG (Camden, NJ); for our National Churches of the Living God, CLG; and for the Living Hope Christian Center, (Willingboro, NJ). She is a much sought after 'Guest' Director for various church Unity and Women's Day Choirs. Carole has three (3) children, Stephanie, Kyanna, and Keith, Jr., who all display musical gifting vocally, mostly in the realm of P&W, also in Audio-Visual Ministry. Carole has three grandsons, Aaron, Semaj and Mehkhi; and a son-in-law, J.P. Heath (Stephanie), who is a psalmist and Praise and Worship Leader. He has recently released his first worship cd titled, *'Appreciate.'*

Byron Anthony Joseph Ward

Born on October 24, 1960. Of all the siblings, Byron is in my opinion the most naturally talented and spiritually gifted in his command of music. He started playing the drums in 1972 at Faith Tabernacle, and later without formal training, started playing the organ. He emerged from a teen inquisitively and clumsily tickling the ivories on the church organ at Faith Tabernacle, to an anointed and inordinately gifted musician. And, Byron can play anything! Give him a mere few minutes to fool around with an instrument and before you know it, he's playing it! That is clearly a gift from God!!! As a keyboardist extraordinaire and master artist on the organ, Byron served as bandleader, composer, arranger, organist and conductor of the Wagner Alumni Choir and played on all of their 4 albums. He has conducted bands in Germany and in Japan. He has traveled with me to Texas, New Orleans, Florida, and at least ten (10) other states throughout the United States. Like June Bug, Lorraine, and Carole, Byron has accepted his call into the preaching ministry.

He is married to Cassandra Edwards of Springfield, Massachusetts. They have two (2) children, Cassandra (Sandy) and Byron, Jr.

These are my siblings and their families. We all came from a pair of dynamite preachers who wanted to please the LORD and lived a life of holiness before us. They recognized that the *'sound of God'* is far greater than the sounds of the prince of darkness – there is no comparison. I thank God for them, for their recognition of the *'sound of God,'* and their determination to introduce us to it, for it has made a difference in our lives, our children's lives, and I trust that it will continue to do so for generations to come.

Chapter Four

"My Children"

A Generation of Levites Continued

On June 3, 1972 I married a trumpet player who lived across the street from my house in West Philadelphia at 5024 Pine Street. His name was Lawrence 'Larry' Farmer. A good looking boy from a Catholic family who attended West Catholic High School, found a Pentecostal girl who was not only a virgin, but had just finished college and ready to receive her first teaching job at Wagner Jr. High School, in the Logan section of Philadelphia. On December 8, 1973, our firstborn, a daughter whom we named **'Larita Lauren,'** arrived. Her birth would be indicative of her life. She was what many would say was a perfect baby. She only cried when she was hungry, and she slept so well that I could sleep. By the time she was two (2) months old, she was sleeping all night. And, by the time Larita was two months shy of turning two years old, she was joined by a little sister, **'Benita,'** on September 26, 1975. By contrast to Larita, Benita wanted to be heard, held, and pampered. Nonetheless, I was so proud of these two beautiful girls that for many years I dressed them as twins. If Larita wore a size 6, I got the same outfit in a size 4 for Benita. But then, by the time the girls reached sizes upwards of 8, Benita learned that her six-year reign as 'the baby' was over. So, now I, Larry, and the girls welcomed another daughter, **'Sharita Joy.'**

Sharita Joy was born on August 18, 1981. This was a special year for me and my husband because this was the year that the Wagner Alumni Choir recorded its first album, on June 6, 1981. I was seven (7) months pregnant with her when I recorded that year *'Wait On The LORD,' 'Afterwhile,' 'Peace In Heaven,'* and *'He Wants To Use You,'* with Sweet Rain Records. By the time of her new sister's arrival, our eldest daughter Larita was months shy of her eighth birthday and was already displaying rhythm in keeping the beat and singing all of our songs. At first, I couldn't tell how or if Benita could sing or not – she was just six years old. And, although I was satisfied with my three (3) beautiful girls as they were, I admit that I had hopes of them being the *'Clark Sisters'* of Philadelphia.

So, what did they do? Larita, Benita, and their cousin Neka, at ages 9, 7, and 11 respectively, did what I'd quietly hoped for – they sang the Clark Sister's song, "Oh, What He's Done For Me," and they did it well! They sang this song while members of the Children's Choir at Faith Tabernacle, conducted by Neka's mother, my cousin Shirley (McDougald). And, they came into their own singing this and other songs, mesmerizing congregation(s) with their harmonies. These kids could sing! Nonetheless, I still wasn't sure how seriously they took singing. But, by the time Larita reached her teenage years at 13, Benita was 10 1/2 and Sharita was 5. It was then that I began to notice that the girls indeed displayed voices to really sing and could maintain harmony as well.

By 1983, my fourth and final child, a son, was born. We wanted a namesake for my husband so badly, but we'd accepted the fact that thus far the LORD had chosen to give us daughters. So, imagine our special joy at this birth, finally – a son! We of course named him Lawrence after his father. He is actually *Lawrence IV, but we call him Larry, Jr.* and initially for many years, *'Little Larry.'* Again, my husband and I were so happy that we finally had a boy after having had three girls. No more hair to comb and braid. And, we got a breather with this one. Like his eldest sister Larita, Little Larry was an easy child to raise and care for. And, by the time he was three (3), Sharita, five (5), Benita, eleven (11), and Larita, thirteen (13), there was no doubt in my mind that I had a musical brood who understood and appreciated the *'sound of music!'*

By the time *Larita* reached the eighth grade, we'd moved the family across the bridge from Philadelphia into New Jersey to the small town of Delran. It was here that it was confirmed that my children had truly inherited the ministry of the Levites. *Larita* chose the drums and percussion instruments as her interest. She would become the first African American female drummer in her High School's history and was inducted into Delran High's Music Hall of Fame. She is today the mother of a teenage son, *DeShawn*, who is displaying his Levitical heritage most recently as a keyboardist and organist. Throughout Elementary School, however, DeShawn played horns (saxophone) in the school band, following in the footsteps of his grandfather, my husband Larry, a trumpeteer.

Benita is today a recording artist who has recorded three projects of her own to date. She sang background vocals on recordings with gospel artist Maurette Brown Clark and inspirational music artist Keith Rovere. Her third and most recent project, 'Mender of Me' is of such healing value that it is already getting wide acclaim, even on social media. She has shared the stage with other great artists such as: Tye Tribbett; William McDowell; Yolanda Adams; Tonex; Eric Roberson and Fred Hammond. Ebony Magazine has noted Benita as one of the Best New Artist in Black Music. In addition to this national recognition, the state of New Jersey previously noted Ms. Farmer as their "Top Independent Female Vocalist".

She graduated with a degree in Music Education from the prestigious Boyer School of Music and Dance at Temple University in Philadelphia. She is presently teaching music at the Creative Arts Morgan Village Academy in Camden, NJ. She has been to Prague, San Juan, Puerto Rico, Nassau, Bahamas, and across the USA, most recently to Nashville, Tennessee, where she led her school choir to victory in taking *'the gold'* in all six categories of a national competition for schools called The Heritage Festival, one of a number of musical festivals held throughout the United States where middle school and high school-aged musical ensembles are ranked on an international standard. These groups include choirs, bands, and orchestras.

Her talents as a teacher and artist have taken her to numerous places and given her an opportunity to minister the Gospel through music wherever she goes. She is the National Assistant Minister of Music for the National Churches of The Living God, and also serves as the Minister of Music for Faith Tabernacle, where I am Pastor.

Sharita Joy doesn't play an instrument, but she has a sweet soprano voice that she is a bit shy about displaying, simply because she doesn't know just how sweet her voice is. Sharita minimizes her ability to sing, but she is yet gifted. She presently lives in North Jersey with her husband, Thorn Hyppolite. They have three (3) beautiful children – Thorn, Jr (TJ), Jolie Ann (JoJo), and Jimmy, aka 'Costello.' In case you're wondering, yes, they all love music and they all have rhythm, even at ages 6, 4, and 2 respectively!

A glimpse of the genius of my youngest, *Larry, Jr.* aka the *'Black Surfer,'* can be seen on the internet in his philosophical and intellectual views. Beyond that, his genus runs the gamut of style as a composer, arranger, and producer of instrumental and vocal projects. He was a drum major in his all-White school band, and played in his

I'm Still Singing

school's competitions for his last two years there. But, it would be the organ that would become the instrument of his passion.

Larry was given his first opportunity to play the organ at a CLG Music Conference under the supervision of Rev. Penny Herndon of Harrisburg, PA. She was the Director of the National Youth Choir at the time. Everyone, including my husband and I were astonished that Larry could play for the choir. Some of his achievements to date are:

1. Played in Japan
2. Played in Italy
3. Played for and traveled with Ty Tribett to England, Amsterdam (Holland), Africa, Canada, and New York, California, and other cities throughout the U.S.
4. Co-produced one of his sister Benita's cd projects.
5. Recorded his own instrumental piece
6. Produced two gospel musical productions
7. At sea for six months playing and providing music on the Carnival Cruise Ship
8. Serves as the House Musician for Faith Tabernacle, CLG

Larry, Jr. is married to Sabrina, herself a musician – a bassist. They have one (1) child, a daughter, Princess Arianna. It should be no surprise to anyone that she sings and plays the violin. She is 6 years old.

Needless to say, I'm still singing through my offspring. I don't know where my children and grandchildren will be tomorrow, but I do believe that they will always have a song that will keep them singing.

Chapter Five

"Musical Influences"

Although I started singing in the public eye at the tender age of four years old in the City of Philadelphia, aka the City of Brotherly Love, my God-given talent was not the only impact that guided my life in music. But, it was various influences that affected my thirst, my drive, my skill, and yes, my spirit to sing Gospel music throughout the world. The following people touched my life and led me towards a path of singing, and singing with a purpose and later with an anointing.

Foremost: It started with my mother, Lillian Ward. Proverbs 31:18 speaks about a virtuous woman. It says that, *"She perceiveth that her merchandise is good: her candle goeth not out by night."* I did not know this fact when I was born, but I realize now that I was my mother's merchandise!

I was born on a sunny day. In fact, it was Labor Day, September 5, 1950, at Temple University Hospital in the heart of North Philadelphia, in the state of Pennsylvania. My mother, Lillian McDougald Ward, and my father, Rev. Edward, Sr., were excited that they had a baby girl, Barbara Ann, after having their first child, a boy, Edward Ward, Jr. They lovingly nicknamed their firstborn 'June Bug', because he was born in the month of June. My parents felt that they had the perfect family. They had a boy with long hair and a beautiful chocolate skin tone whom everyone adored (particularly our grandparents), and now some 15 months later, they greeted to the Ward Clan with equal joy and excitement, a 7 lbs. baby girl with hardly any hair at all! So, I was known as the *'cute little clean-head baby'*, as my late Aunt Jessie Mae frequently and endearingly referenced me. My mother who was herself the youngest of her siblings in a family of six (6), had at this point outnumbered all of them in the child-bearing category with two (2) children by the end of 1950. Ten years later, the number of Ward children would have increased by four as this soon to be musical family of South Philadelphia developed.

Growing up in South Philadelphia or 'South Philly' as it was frequently called in the 50's, was a unique time to live. The trolley cars were still rolling then; cheese steaks, hoagies ('subs' or 'heros' to people in other regions), tasty-kake, Italian water ice, yum-yums (a smoother, creamier, less icy version of water ice), and cracker jacks, comprised the prominent cuisine of South Philly, at least to a child. But, the whole country experienced *'a taste of Philadelphia'* through its impact on music in the secular scene, with names such as *Chubby Checker, Frankie Avalon, Fabian, Dee Dee Sharpe, Dick Clark and American Bandstand,* which aired from Philadelphia and put it on the musical map (in the 60's and 70's Philadelphia's musical popularity would grow so much that it would even develop its own signature of soul music called the *'Philly Sound'* or *'Sound of Philadelphia'*). And, there was the Philadelphia Arena, a popular venue for special events, located at 46th & Market Streets near the tracks of the 'El', or the city's elevated train system. Concurrently, in our small house in 1951, my mom told me that my maternal grandmother looked at me while I was standing up in my crib, and staring out into the room, she said, **"Lillian, that girl is going to be a singer."** Now, how she knew that remains a mystery to all of us because she never called herself a prophetess or soothsayer. But, by the time I was 4 yrs. old, and with two (2) more children added to the family by 1954, my mother had me singing boldly, and fearlessly in packed churches, and 'packed houses' all around the city of Philadelphia.

My mother told me that while I was still a toddler she sang to me around the house throughout the day and then again at bedtime. She knew that some talent was brewing within me because I started singing back to her. My first song as a toddler was, *"Jesus, I Love You for Your Tender Care."* I was told that although my pronunciation was definitely childish or 'cutesy', that I had good pitch and good tones, and could imitate my mother or anyone else around me who could sing.

By the time I turned 5 yrs. old, I was known throughout the city as *'Little Miss 5 years old Barbara Ann Ward.'* My mother had me singing at many churches throughout the city, and it was a time when *'child stars'* were popping up everywhere. My contemporaries were *Little Larry Hood, Sandra Peyton, the Beck Brothers, The Ranges Trio, from Chester, PA., The Sapp Sisters, and the 'Twins',* who'd later sing on the Philadelphia Mass Choir (80's) and who now sing on the Victory Choral Ensemble. These child singers as well as I sang at the old Cornerstone Baptist Church, the old Oak Grove Baptist Church, the Churches of the Living God (CLG) National Temple, and at the popular Ranges Temple, in Chester, PA.

Now, the amazing thing about my early years of singing from 1954–1961 was that at the age of 7, the church community still labeled me as *'Little Miss 5 yrs. old Barbara Ann Ward.'* This went on until I was about 9 years of age. I guess it was because of my height and size. You see, although I sounded like a 10-year-old, I looked like I was age 5. The second amazing thing was that during the 50's in Philadelphia, there was the emergence of the first 'Divas' appearance in gospel music – a mother and daughters, that began to move this genre of music to a national level, with their specialty in singing style, hair-do's, and forms of outrageous attire. This group was called, *Clara Ward and the Ward Singers*! This singing group was managed by Clara's mom, *Madame Gertrude Ward*. They were highly distinguished among the Philadelphia circuit of singers because they were the first *'gospel'* group to appear on national television, the first in the area to ride around in limousines, and the first and only gospel group to hold their anniversary celebration at the Philadelphia Arena, then located at 46th & Market Streets. This was definitely a step up for gospel because the Arena housed secular acts and for a long time was the home of the nationally syndicated, 'American Bandstand.'

Now, my mother told me that when Madame Gertrude Ward heard there was a little girl child in the city with the same last name as hers and Clara's who could really sing, she thought it would be a smart gesture to promote me as her relative (niece or grandchild, I'm not sure which). Thus, at their anniversary celebration in 1959, I believe, at the Philadelphia Arena, I was invited to sing before a crowd of 11, 000!!! Sing, I did, along with my sister, Brenda, who we called *'Brenda Doll'* because she was the prettier one. But, I was the singer – she was my back up (smile)! I was nine and she was seven. We sang, *'I Want Jesus To Walk With Me!'* We were a sensational hit as the little *'Ward'* children.

At this time, the late *Marion Williams* and *Kitty Parham* were now members of the sensational Ward Singers. I remember seeing Marion Williams at the Arena singing, *'Packing Up, Getting Ready To Go!'* Friends, this was a sight to behold, even as a child. Mother Williams, as I later would call her, sang, pranced about, and literally picked up and packed up as many pocketbooks as she possibly could as she strolled throughout the Arena singing this song with a delightful ferocity (actually, I was afraid of her when she sang this song. For some reason, I thought that if she looked at me, I'd be the next thing she'd pack up).

"The Philadelphia Scene"

After this association with the Ward Singers, as I recall, my name as a child singer began to spread even more throughout the Philadelphia region. I remember singing at the *Philadelphia Met* at Broad & Poplar Streets, in North/Central Philadelphia. It was here that many of the greatest gospel artists from around the country performed at ticketed programs on special nights such as Easter Monday, Thanksgiving, and at various times when promoters held a 'Gospel Show' in the 50's and 60's. This promotion was done by way of publications, brightly documented placards, flyers, and billboards advertising who was about to appear. It was nothing for a little singer youngster such as myself to open up to massive crowds at this massive theater type building for such groups as *The Swanee Quintet, The Soul Stirrers, The Dixie Hummingbirds, The Highway Q.C.'s, The Five Blind Boys (of Alabama and Mississippi);* or for the many dynamic female gospel groups such as *The Roberta Martin Singers, The Caravans,* and *Dorothy Love Coates and the Gospel Harmonettes.* Sometimes at the Met, Philadelphia or New Jersey area artists performed, electrifying me even as a child, because they sang hard, were very demonstrative, and crossed the line from classical spirituals to getting down, dancing and rejoicing, foot stomping, gospel singing that were both spirited and uplifting. Groups such as *Rudolf Lewis and the Newberry Singers, The Thompson Sisters, The Gospel Clefs,* and later *The Gospel Imperials and The Stars of Faith,* were groups that I remember that had an effect on me both at the Met and at the largest churches in the Philadelphia area. These groups and those that I'll mention later had an effect on me with their different styles of singing, their delivery of the songs, and their conduct *'off stage'* so to speak, that made a lifetime impact on me that still exists today.

Bishop Dr. Barbara Ward Farmer

"On The Radio"

In the late 50's, live radio was the way to go for people to hear you, particularly if you had not ever recorded. My mother would wake me up early in the morning and give me some warm sugar water to drink so that my voice would be clear and fresh for the live performance on the radio. WHAT and WDAS were the Philadelphia black community's primary radio stations in the 50's and 60's. Here, I was encouraged by radio personalities that made a good impression on me, boosting my self-confidence and vocal prowess, which eventually helped me as a teenager. During the gospel show hours, DJ's like the very highly esteemed Mary Dee, and later her daughter Bonnie Dee, talked to me and gave me the opportunity to sing on their morning program. Later, Mary Mason and her protégé, Brother Walter Stewart, lit up the airways with the soulful sounds of gospel music. During the secular radio program hours there were Kay Williams and Georgie Woods, who dominated the *'devil's music'*, as we *'holy and sanctified'* people used to call this kind of music. I later learned this signified that it was music that did not glorify God. And, my mother was steadfast in steering me clear of 'the devil's music.' <u>An illustration of my mother's commitment and example of holiness to me is in a well-known family story</u>: *My mother's famous story about me in those early radio years is that when I was about nine or ten years old, Mr. Kay Williams (one of the secular spin-masters or DJ's), upon hearing me sing, thought that I had the potential of then 'Little Stevie Wonder' from Detroit, who was starting to get recognition as a child 'wonder' in the country. So, it is reported that Mr. Williams asked my mother to have me switch from singing gospel to singing secular music. He further told her that "because I was a child, I would sing in only the best night clubs and theaters, and that he could promise her **$500.00 a week** (for starters), if she would allow me to sing under his management." Now remember,* *this is the late 1950's. Five hundred dollars was a lot of money for a poor family of 5 in South Philly. So, what was my mom's response? She told me that the Holy Ghost spoke to her almost immediately and she answered him and said,* **"No! What will it profit a man to gain the whole world and then lose his soul? No, sir. I can't do it!"** *Needless to say, Mr. Williams thought that my mom was crazy. But, now, hallelujah, I'm still singing songs for God, songs that elevate Jesus! I believe that remaining on the path of purpose spared me heartache and pain. I've never been on drugs but I'm high because of His death and the power of His resurrection.*

Chapter Six

"Why Am I Different?"

Along with my dear mother, Lillian Ward, who at the time in 1959 had not yet accepted her calling into the preaching ministry until after my baby brother, Byron, was born in 1960, I realized that I was different. Different in that I knew that I could sing, because the people told me that I could. I saw their reaction every time they called on me as *'Little Miss Barbara Ann Ward'* or *'Little Five-Year-Old Barbara Ann Ward.'* Again, by the time I reached ten, I was still so short that they continued to call me *'Five-Year-Barbara Ann Ward.'* And, by 1956, I had an anniversary every year. My mom had posters or placards as they called them in the '50's that whenever there was an anniversary or a great event those placards were staple-gunned to utility poles throughout the city as free advertisement in the city. My mother made sure that I was well-grounded after every performance, singing engagement, and every event that could easily express the 'star' treatment.

Somewhere between the ages of 8 and 11, my family and I had transitioned from my grandfather's church in South Philadelphia to a church in a small south jersey town called Penns Grove, where the pastor was a woman. Yes, a woman! My mother had heard of women pastors and preachers because she had seen the likes of late-greats Mother Dabney, Bishop Bessie Washington, and of course, Bishop

Ida Robinson. But, at that time she had no personal knowledge or contact with one. So, when someone told her about a woman pastor named Elder Linda Colene Williams, she was drawn to her church in Penns Grove, NJ where she (Elder Williams) had been sent by her leader in the Churches of the Living God, Bishop A.H. White. My mother, being a woman of faith who strived to only 'walk in the steps the LORD ordered for her' knew that this woman pastor was someone she had to meet because it was destined and ordained to be so. This transition would prove to be even more significant than my mother could imagine for all of us. As for me, it was the beginning of the *first step* in my life as a singer.

Still feeling the impact of being different because I could sing, I started to feel like I had to prove that I was like everybody else – normal. I sang in the school's Glee Club, I sang at funerals, I sang at weddings, and I wasn't even yet a teenager! Everyone in the neighborhood knew me. Some of the girls even said unkind things about me, i.e. "She thinks she's cute." This was troubling to me because these accusations and feelings of being special were so untrue. However, I did feel different. I never told my mother about these feelings, but by age 11, I really wanted to fit in with everybody else.

Our new church in Penns Grove as well as my parents' standards taught me about holiness. That meant that we didn't smoke, drink, curse, dance worldly dances, or listen to secular music like the blues, jazz, or rock'n'roll. There was no such thing as hip hop or rap in the late 50's and early '60's, but I'm sure that if there was, it would've been included in this restriction.

As a child singer, nobody told me that I was different, but I knew that I was because of my upbringing and because of the notoriety of being a 'child star' in the hood. The music my mother gave me to sing was not music that intimidated anyone (besides the devil), for it was purely Gospel. At some point, I began to understand the difference between holiness and secular singing. Holiness brings about a special deliverance. You sing what you feel, and you feel the essence of the *'sound of God'* that is personified in holiness. As a child, I began to grasp this concept, and over the years learned to embrace and hold onto it. God has proven this truth to me time and time again.

By 1960, my mother started to accept her call into the preaching ministry, and in October of that year my baby brother Byron was born. By then I had written my first song. What was to come would change my feelings about 'difference' into a sense of 'purpose.'

Chapter Seven

'The Impact of Salvation'

"Recording For The First Time"

From 1954 to 1960, I had the privilege and honor to sing throughout the Philadelphia and Chester, PA areas, various New Jersey cities, Brooklyn, NY, and the Boston, Massachusetts area. In 1961, I was a member of Holy Temple Church of the Living God, in Penns Grove, N.J., where the late Bishop L.C. Williams was my pastor. Her daughter, Garnita Selby, was my godmother. This association had a great impact on me because this relationship along with my mom gave me the confidence to sing boldly even if I didn't understand completely the significance of what I was singing about. Earlier that same year (1961), my mother entered me into a gospel singing contest – and I won! I was 10 ½ years old at the time. The prize was a recording contract with *Revelations Records* out of New York City. Needless to say, my genetic family, my pastor and church family, were very excited about this new stage in my life as a potential recording artist. By September of that year when I turned 11, my godmother, Garnita, introduced me to *Evangelist Rosie Wallace of the Gospel Imperials of Philadelphia*. Evangelist Wallace, a popular singer, musician, superb songwriter and prolific arranger of the day, wrote two songs that I would eventually record on my first recording.

In 1961, people recorded albums on plastic or vinyl as what was called *33rmp's (33's)*, or smaller circular vinyl records that held a single song on each side of it. These were called *45's (45 rpm's)*. The acronym *'rpm'* signifies *'revolutions per minute'*, or *'rotations per minute'*, which defined the speed at which the phonograph or record spun the record around. *I made a 45.* For you younger crowd, that's the record that has an 'A' and 'B' side, with the doughnut hole in the middle and is played on a 'phonograph' machine or 'record player'. Well, later that year, my godmother took me to a New York studio where in an isolation booth I recorded, *'By The Grace of God'*, and *'What Do You Think About Jesus?'*

I realize when I look back now at that first studio experience in New York, I was exposed to several things that would positively impact me later in my recording life:

1. My first experience with a live studio band backing me up
2. Although the band and I were in the same room, I was isolated from everyone else, with my own microphone.
3. My first time experiencing what I call a "dead mic" (microphone). I saw the mic, but I couldn't really hear myself.
4. The organist at the time was a young lady whom I later learned was Dr. Becky Carlton. Dr. Carlton was at that time a studio musician from New York. She would later gain notoriety as the 'Queen of the Hammond Organ,' and would relocate to Philadelphia where she would reside until her death in 2010, serving as Co-Pastor and Minister of Music at the Sanctuary Church of the Open Door. My initial encounter with her would turn out to be a lifetime acquaintance with her and even her daughter who had not yet been born, Dr. Kim Carlton.

Needless to say, this was a totally awesome experience for me as an eleven year old who had never recorded before. When the 45 was released months later, it received raving reviews and an awful lot of air play in the Philadelphia area. D.J.'s Mary Dee and daughter Bonnie Dee really loved the project and promoted it beyond our wildest dreams. And it was during these pre-teen years that I experienced singing gospel of course, at the *Uptown Theater in Philadelphia,* and the renowned *Apollo Theatre in New York*, at one of their infamous *'Amateur Nights.'* There were events in my life that I don't talk much about because <u>meaning, purpose, and Spirit had no significance for me at the time.</u> But, I was after this recording, a child sensation who was getting ready to know Jesus personally!

Where The Spirit Met The Song

All through my neighborhood at 2624 Ellsworth Street and at Benson Elementary School at 27th and Wharton Streets, where I was getting ready to leave for Audenreid Jr. High School at 33rd & Tasker Sts., the word was out that a South Philly kid made a record singing gospel music. Indeed, I was a great imitator and interpreter of music as I knew it at 11 years of age. But there was something missing that occurred to me at this point in my young life. I sang the message, but could not really translate its significance in my life. For it was at this point in my young life that I started to *'notice'*: I *noticed* boys, I *noticed* meaning, and I *noticed* that my music was robotic – I did as I'd seen others do, and I did as I was told, but could not connect to or translate a real existence of God for myself. Now, I know this may seem strange since I came from a Christian home with a marvelous, hardworking father, and an assertive and supportive mom (who at this point had accepted her own call into the public ministry). But, in March 1962, I *noticed* – realized, there was a missing link that was evident.

It was around this time that I began to have a desire to play the piano. We were too poor to own a piano, but my Aunts Alice and Jessie Mae had a piano in their house. I wanted to play so much that I would walk for at least ½ mile to their house at 24th & Catherine Street and taught myself to play in every key. Consequently, it was also around the early 60's that I wrote my first song for my sisters and me entitled, *'With The Help of God.'* We still sing this song when we get together after all of these years.

Our church in Penns Grove, NJ, was having one of its many revivals (I got converted at least 5 times in each revival at the church that I can remember). But, this revival in 1962 was different. I didn't know it then, but I now know that I was really hungry for God, for real. I realized that I needed to be saved. Just a few months before, an Elder from one of our Church of Living God churches in Florida, Elder Green, said something to me that affected me in that 1962 revival at Penns Grove. Elder Green said these words: *"Barbara Ann, you have a beautiful voice. But, if you get saved, you could really sing sho'nuff!"* Well, this floored me, because I thought that I was already *'really singing.'* I mean, I had all the right moves and mimicked what I saw the adult gospel singers do. So, these words bothered me for months leading up to that March night in 1962 when I did something about it.

Back in the 1960's, we believed in *tarrying* for the Holy Ghost. Especially when there was a revival, you got to know what that actually meant. Because, whenever there was a revival, *tarrying* was in full force. Although the Holy Ghost could be sought for, or tarried for, at anytime and anywhere, some folks excitedly looked forward to revival just so they could *tarry* for Him. This was in accordance with the intensity and high energy of the spirit reminiscent of the Azusa Street Revivals, which is credited as the birth of the Pentecostal movement where crowds gathered for days – singing, praying, writhing in the Spirit, and speaking in tongues. So, in the Pentecostal faith, revival meant electricity was in the air; shouting, dancing, and hearing chants throughout the congregation of: "Hallelujah!" "Thank You Jesus!" "You got it!" "Hold on!" "Don't let go!" There was copious *'speaking in unknown tongues'* or *'glossolalia,'* – heavenly language that no one understands, which was considered as a 'sure' sign that you'd received the Baptism of the Holy Ghost that accompanied this electricity or fire. The clapping of hands, the sweat pouring from one's face, the spit or 'purging' as the old folks used to call it, were also a part of the revival experience that came from hours and hours of *'tarrying'* repeating, "Jesus, Jesus, Jesus!" The goal was to get a breakthrough and receive the promise recorded in Acts 1:8 – *"But you shall receive power when the Holy Spirit has come upon you; and you shall be witnesses to Me in Jerusalem, and in all Judea and Samaria, and to the end of the earth."*

And so, on that wintry evening of 1962, my Pentecostal upbringing had somewhat prepared me for what was to happen next. The revival began on Monday and ended on Friday night. After crying, praying, and praising God all week, by Friday the Holy Ghost came in, changed my tongue – I began to speak and I knew from the moment God filled me with His precious Spirit that this time I had the Holy Ghost and the Holy Ghost had me! When I opened my eyes, I knew that the link that was missing was the link with God, and He had connected Himself with my soul and spirit and brought about a *'new me'* that affected the way I thought, the way I interacted with people, and most of all, the way that I sang. Indeed, after my Day of Pentecost experience, my singing began to change. The Holy Ghost began to translate for me. What impact God's grace had on me! *'What Do You Think About Jesus?'* became my testimony of what I *really* thought about my Savior.

Bishop Dr. Barbara Ward Farmer

"From Singing To Ministry"

In September 1962, I started the 7th grade at Audenreid Jr. High School. Everything about me was *'new' – new* school, *new* grade, *new* acquaintances, and *a new life in Christ*. Like in elementary school, the gift of music always shaped my musical abilities to perform, listen, and produce sounds taught to me. I had two experiences that shaped my musical talents at this point in my life – **a school** expanding my musical awareness, and **a church** also expanding my musical awareness. From Mrs. Blackwell in elementary school; Mr. Nelson, Mr. Colon (from Trinidad), and Ms. Clark from Audenreid; to Mr. Yeats at South Philadelphia High, my musical experiences shaped and 'developed my ears' for the expected sounds and tones involving the pitch, dynamic, and presentation that every performer should have. However, it was the Holy Ghost that I received at the revival at my church that 'shaped my heart' and my passion for Christ. I had learned classical pieces, dynamics, rhythm, pitch, and how to direct choral music from my musical experiences in glee clubs, school choirs and musicals, and plays, from 1962-1968. God gave me favor to audition for and to participate in the *'Philadelphia All City High Schools Choir'* in 1967 and 1968. This was a prestigious honor earned by the most talented and gifted High School students within the entire city. We performed classical pieces at the prestigious *Academy of Music* and at the *Philadelphia Spectrum* with the *All City Orchestra* before thousands of people.

However, unlike my performances as a soloist before 1962, my view and feeling about music were now forever changed. God was now the reason, basis, and foundation for why and how I viewed music. In church, I continued to sing throughout my organization within the Churches of the Living God's *'White Dominion,'* (which extended from Massachusetts to Florida, and from New Jersey to Ohio) at the various conventions and assemblies up to 1968. In 1967,

I'm Still Singing

at the age of 16, I re-recorded Evangelist Rosie Wallace's *'By The Grace of God',* with the *CLG National Foreign Mission Choir,* in Harrisburg, PA. This recording was live, and now at age 16 *and* filled with the Holy Ghost, I knew something about God's grace. So now, my delivery of the song as I remember, was message-driven into real ministry. This album was the very first recording for the National Church and a success for it.

My influences within the CLG organization were many. The following individuals influenced how I heard music and how I interpreted it from a spiritual viewpoint of **singing with the anointing** – that is, *the supernatural Divine ability to accomplish what one does when one goes forth to accomplish it.* These saints were my choir directors or organists who gave me a chance to sing from the age of ten to eighteen when I entered college in 1968: Professor Edward G. Robinson, Detroit, MI.; Brothers Jerry and Benny Drone, Akron, OH.; Elder Ruth Dennison, Philadelphia, PA.; Bishop Leila Jenkins, Philadelphia, PA.; Brother William Marshall, Springfield, MA.; and Attorney Garnita Selby, Philadelphia, PA., who was my very first choir director in Penns Grove, N.J. The late Jimmy Smith, Bernard Chandler and Jimmy Washington, all of Philadelphia, were my accompanists during my early solo years. Each of these young men was like a big brother and instructor to me. I shall never forget their love, caring, and influence in shaping my career as a young child singer.

It was during my teen years that the Gospel world had some of the greatest songwriters, singers, arrangers, and musicians that certainly had a lasting affect on me and my soon to be developed style of singing, teaching, and directing vocalists and choirs during my college days and well into the 70's. The following people gave a Holy Ghost-filled style of singing and performing that excited me because that's the type of ministry that I wanted to be involved with. National and international legends and greats such as the late *Dr.*

Mattie Moss Clark from the Church of God In Christ, had a style that was uniquely hers, and for me transformed the sound of the church choir into a power packed ministry of heaven on earth. A young man from the *Bibleway Church of the Apostolic Church of the Lord Jesus,* by the name of *Michael Rogers,* wrote one song, *'Stay With God,'* that changed my choral thinking with possibilities that went beyond the church into a variation of changes and patterns that were certainly different for the times. The late-great *Reverend James Cleveland* emerged for me as the primary *anybody can sing this song* Sunday choir writer and arranger.

In the mid 60's I believe, my godmother took a few young people to Washington, D.C., to attend *UNEC,* which was COGIC's (Church of God In Christ) National Youth and Music Conference in which I saw for the first time, a choir that called themselves the *Northern California Choir.* It was at one of those COGIC's *'A Song Is Born'* services, where choirs competed for the best song, best performance, and best delivery. The winner was this Northern California Choir dressed in white tops and black bottoms. That was the first time that I saw or heard *Edwin Hawkins* and his younger brother *Walter Hawkins.* They gave the performance of their lives! They had a soloist that blew us all away with her range and delivery reach. I found out later that her name was *Tramaine Davis.* She would later marry Walter and establish the Hawkins Family tradition in the gospel world. Their name today is immediately recognizable, even legendary, for its indelible effect and influence on the industry and ministry of gospel music.

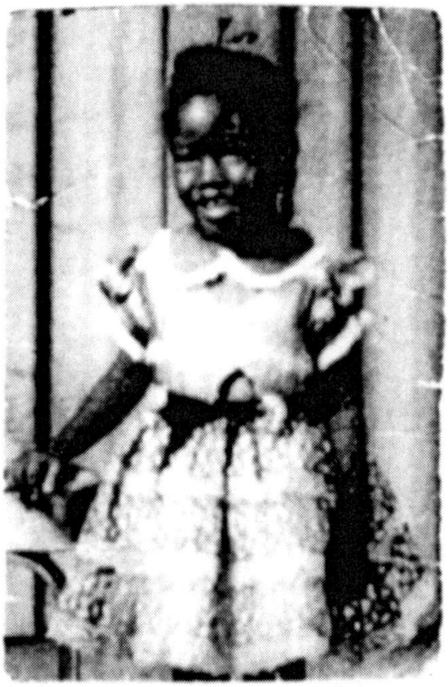

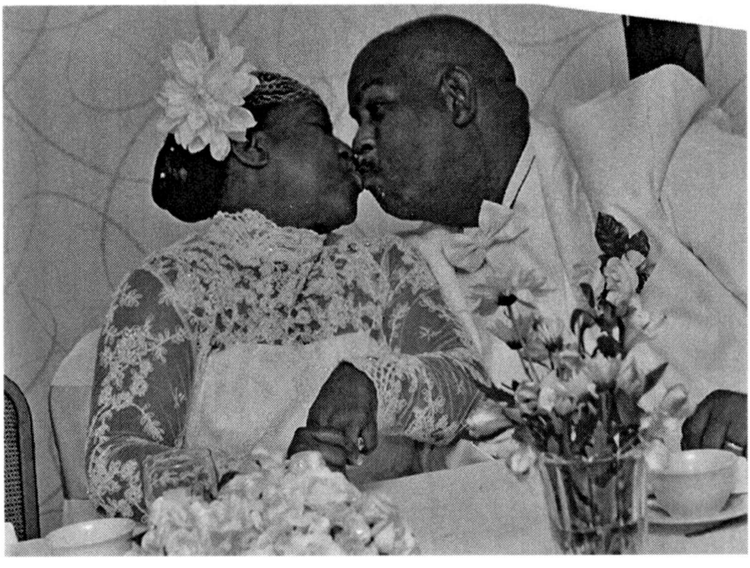

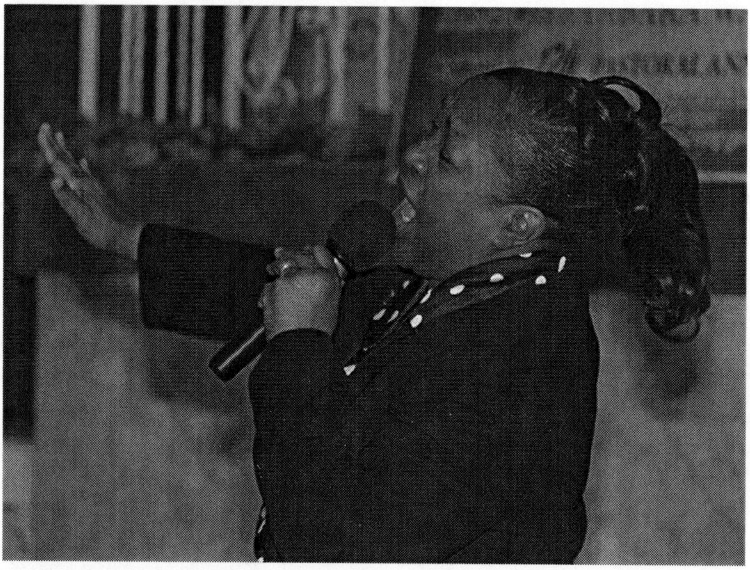

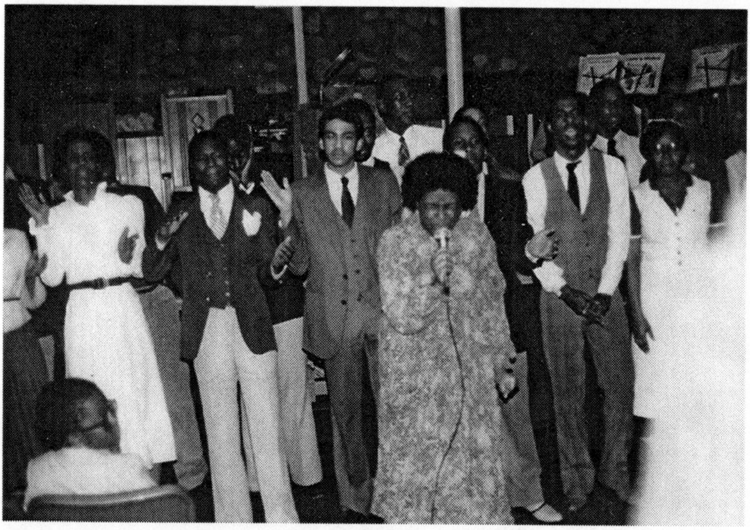

Mother....

Sister / Daughter....

Look What God Has Done Over the Years!

Pastor....    *Wife....*

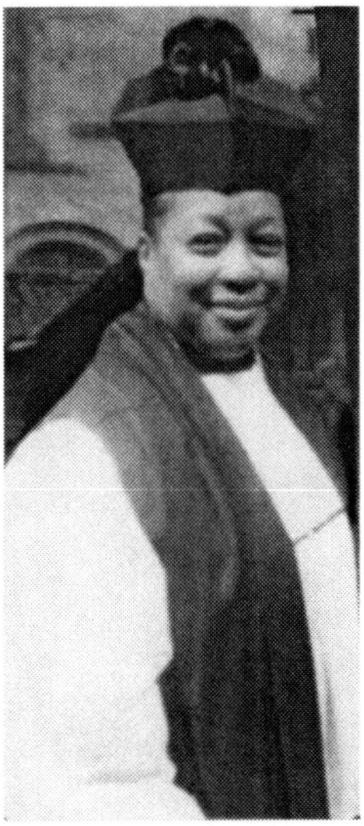

Chapter Eight

"New Journey, New Experiences"

In 1968, I began my life as a collegiate at West Chester State, a small teachers' college in Pennsylvania. This was an exciting time for me because I was the first in the Ward Clan to attend college and I was extremely proud to represent my family and church as a Spanish Language major. While living on campus, I learned to be independent and I kept my salvation. In 1969, my mother starting pastoring in *Camden, N.J.,* and I had mixed emotions about our move (in membership) from Penns Grove, N.J. to another town in New Jersey, right across the bridge from Philadelphia, in fact, called *Camden.* Nonetheless, every weekend I came home from college, soon finding myself at another stage in my life – that of Minister of Music for a new church. While a student in college, I had to learn how to form a choir, and how to conduct *Devotional Services,* or what we today call *Praise and Worship* – all before 1980. This was indeed a tremendous transition for me and my family because we left a well-established, Word-based, musical church and came to a storefront on *'Broadway',* a strip in Camden, where my mother was the only minister, and my sisters – Brenda, Lorraine, and Carol, and brothers – Edward, Jr. and Byron, and cousins – Jackie and Shirley, formed the first ensemble and musical team at Faith Tabernacle, our new church home.

In the 1970's I taught songs from both Reverend James Cleveland Dr. Mattie Moss Clark; and the Institutional Radio Choir, a choir from Brooklyn, NY whose popularity was mounting at the time. Adding the music of Walter and Edwin Hawkins to the caliber of 70's and 80's popular gospel music that I taught our choir, our church's congregation and music ministry began to grow with me on the organ, my sister Lorraine directing, and my baby brother, Byron, playing the drums. Clearly, the 1970's was the decade of the choir and the *'choir sound.'* While the 40's, 50's, and early 60's were the eras of group music, both male and female, the 70's and 80's were the beginning of the choir sound. Almost every church choir was singing a Reverend James Cleveland tune, a C.O.G.I.C. masterpiece, or a Hawkins work of art.

The *'choir sound'* as I saw it was different from the traditional quartet, and the men and women's groups that were popular pre-1970. These consisted of no more than 5-6 members plus the pianist or organist. Or, in the case of the quartet, usually the four singers were accompanied by a lead guitarist and a drummer. In later times a bassist was added on. The *'choir sound'* however, consisted of a full section of sopranos, altos and tenors, that sang in parts harmoniously, with a full band such as an organist, pianist, drummer, bass and guitar player, and later a horn section. The choir had a director who was usually energetic and even flamboyant in getting everything majestically possible out of as many as 60-80 singers and musicians. A smaller number of voices was often called an 'Ensemble,' while larger numbers of voices with various age groups represented and strong in vocal skills were called 'Mass Choirs.'

In 1970, while still attending college, the Lord inspired me to form the first Gospel Choir at West Chester State. Believe me friends, this was not a real challenge because I had several good things going for me. First of all, God gave us a place on campus in the music department to meet, rehearse, and have our time of fellowship and singing. Second, the choir was the only thing that the Black students could identify to each other with other than the seemingly defunct NAACP. Third, I had an ear for music, and I learned how to teach while playing the piano. *Oh, did I tell you that I could now play the piano?* I learned this art form around 1963 but didn't perfect it until 1969 as a college freshman. It was also at West Chester that I wrote my second and third songs: *'Oh, Son of David Have Mercy On Us!'* and *'Devotion.'*

The West Chester Gospel Choir was popular around campus because God gave us favor to travel to many colleges and churches to spread the Word of God to as many people as possible. My experience here at West Chester State gave me leadership confidence and helped me to understand voices and choral blends. When I graduated from West Chester in May 1972, I was ready for what was to come next musically. A Divine plan unfolded…

I think it is important to tell you what inspired me to form the gospel choir at West Chester. It was during this time that I heard that gospel music had expanded from the pew to the school. Howard University had historically established a reputation for having good choral music for the classics and the spiritual refinement of culture and history. But it was the emergence of the Black Revolution in the country in the late 60's and early 70's that made way for another revolution of sorts – in the church – and that was a transformation from hymns and spirituals to Gospel Music as we know it today. This church music, sung with fervor and emotion, was seen throughout the colleges, universities, and later established in high schools. This unique gospel explosion was experienced also at the junior high (grades 7-9, in those days) and elementary school levels (K-6).

Edwin Hawkins', *O Happy Day,* was gospel's first *'cross over'* music, internationally introducing gospel in a different light. Now, I'm sure there were many people responsible for this church art form appearing at the college level, but it was the sounds at Howard

University under the direction of a young student who would later go on to be known as one of the nation's most prolific and creative songwriters and arrangers by the name of *Richard Smallwood*, that would inspire me to form the Gospel Choir at West Chester. As an added influence, it was Philadelphia's own Gabriel Hardeman *(Gabriel Hardeman Delegation),* a teacher at the Strawberry Mansion Jr. High School (which later became a High School), who inspired me to years later have horn arrangements in most of the Wagner Alumni Choir's albums. He was the first that I'd ever seen to have 'live' horns onstage at a performance.

"1972 – A Year To Remember"

I believe that everybody has a special year that they can recall what is both memorable and eventful. Well, 1972 was that year for me. Let me tell you how my year went:

- *January* – began student teaching at Bartram High School in the Southwest section of the City of Philadelphia.
- *May* – graduated from West Chester State with a Baccalaureate Degree (B.S.) in Secondary Spanish Education. Left the West Chester State Gospel Choir in the capable hands of Esther Wicks, who kept the choir going. In fact, it remains in existence today.
- *June 3rd* – on this day, at 1 p.m., at 22 yrs of age, married my teenage sweetheart, Larry Farmer, who lived right across the street from me growing up. Our wedding was beautifully done by the late Bishop A.H. White, our Presiding Prelate (of the Churches of The Living God – CLG), at our then National Headquarters church at 58th & Thompson Streets, in Philadelphia. My sisters – Lorraine and Carol, and cousins Jackie (Dunlap-Logan) and Judy Coppage, Anita Ward,

I'm Still Singing

sister-in-law, and my dear friend Linda Phillips (whom I'd known since childhood days at Penns Grove), and my college roommate Marla Griffin, were in the wedding. I think it was the wedding of the year because God ordained it from the beginning. Larry and I are still happily married after all these years!

- *1st week of September* – began my first teaching position at Wagner Junior High School in the West Oak Lane section of Philadelphia. I'd received a teacher's grant in 1968 that guaranteed me a teacher's job if I promised to teach in the Philadelphia Public School System upon graduation from college. Here again, God was moving in my life. Thus, needless to say, this job was a blessing from the LORD as He continued to grant me Divine favor in alignment with so many occurrences in my life. For, here in this new position, at this new school, I was given permission to start and organize a gospel choir at the junior high school level! God had knowingly prepared me so that all that was needed was for me to simply incorporate the same skills that I'd acquired at West Chester State at Wagner Junior High, beginning a chapter in the life of the eventually established *Wagner Jr. High School Choir, and later, the Wagner Alumni Choir.*
- *Mid-September* – accepted my call to the preaching ministry, and preached my initial sermon at my home church, Faith Tabernacle, CLG; established by my mother, then Pastor Lillian Ward, at 1224 Broadway Sts., Camden, N.J. The title of the message was, **'The Available Strength of God.'** The scripture was **Psalms 46.**

My new journey and my new experiences after 1972 included a beautiful and fulfilled life which gave me another song to sing. I took pleasure in singing about my years of higher education, and how God brought me through them still saved, sanctified, and singing. Now in a new church with the title of "*First* Family, *First* Organist, and *First* Minister of Music; it fills me with joy to know that at this time in my life I also found love, and love found me – into the arms of my husband and childhood beau, Lawrence "Larry" Farmer. I glorify my God that has favored me to sing an encore of blessings as I went on to get my first teaching job in September 1972, and I glorify the Almighty for allowing me to respond to His will by preaching my initial sermon – all in the same year.

And there's more. On December 8, 1973, once again a new life began for me, one that I yet enjoy even more today than on that day. That day, I sang the praises of God as I embraced *motherhood*. 'Larita Lauren' was born at the prestigious University of Pennsylvania Hospital in Philadelphia, early in the morning by means of natural birth. Motherhood was then and remains a joy for me because I have always had consistent support from my mother, husband, and church members. Not only did I learn how to approach motherhood with joy, but I embraced the LORD's wisdom that guided me in terms of what I should do, and how I was to get along with my husband, how to raise Larita, and later the three (3) more children that we would have, and how to do it still singing.

Chapter Nine

"The Wagner Alumni Choir"

"Recording Again"

Now that I was preaching, I continued to work with the music ministry at my church while teaching at Wagner and getting a lot of exposure throughout the city from the Wagner Gospel Choir. They had won two city-wide competitions as the best Jr. High School Choir in the city, and we purchased over 60 beautiful blue choir robes for the school that were to remain in the school.

In 1976, I left my teaching position at Wagner Jr. High School but the students still wanted to sing together as a group. There were also others outside of the Wagner student body who wanted to sing with them as well. So, around 1977, we began to rehearse at one of the neighborhood churches, Second Macedonia Baptist. It was here that we rehearsed for many years, transforming from *'a school choir'* into a new choir with a new name: *'The Wagner Alumni Choir.'* We traveled to many churches throughout the region. People began to know us as the former school choir who could really sing. Later still, in the late 70's and early 80's, we began rehearsing at the home church of our guitarist, David Bruno, Temple Shalom, on Champlost Street, also in the West Oak Lane Section of Philadelphia. Praise God! Those were the days! By the way, David Bruno now pastors Temple Shalom. Glory be to God!

By 1980, my husband and I already had two (2) beautiful girls: Larita and Benita, who each possessed unmistakably excellent ears for music at a very young age. They developed their father's ability to read music (he played the trumpet at West Catholic High School before he joined my church and Wagner, where, although Gabriel Hardeman was its inspiration, he contributed largely to Wagner's *'horns section'* and signature *'brass'* sound). Meanwhile, our home church under my mother's leadership began to grow so rapidly that we sought a larger building on Spruce Street in Camden, N.J. We purchased a 1,000 seat edifice that became the new home of Faith Tabernacle Church, CLG., and we marched into the building in April of 1979. I continued with the music ministry at the church, forming the *'Ward Ensemble'* as the premier choir of the church.

By the end of 1980, the Wagner Alumni Choir was approached by *Calvin Carr*, a friend of mine from high school, who invited us to record with his partners in their newly formed recording company, *'Sweet Rain Records.'* We consented to record with them as *'Evangelist Barbara Ward Farmer and the Wagner Alumni Choir.'* However, by January 1981, after six years since last giving birth, I discovered that I was pregnant with our third child.

At first, we thought that the recording, scheduled for June, would have to be delayed. The Sweet Rain staff, consisting of *Andrew Ford* (now Bishop Andrew Ford, pastor of the Ford Memorial Church, in Philadelphia, PA); his younger brother and musical genius, *Steven Ford* (now a renowned musical producer and Minister of the Gospel); horn arranger, *Leon Frison* (now a Minister of the Gospel), and musical staff *Calvin Carr* (now a Minister of the Gospel) *Garfield Williams,* (now, 'Elder Williams') and *'Ting' Paul Burke* (now, pastor of the Victory Outreach Center in Philadelphia, PA). There were others who came aboard later, but these men were the hands-on musical talents that helped us create our own musical staff to record our very first album on June 6, 1981, in Philadelphia, PA. I was seven (7) months pregnant singing such songs as *'Wait On the LORD,' 'He Wants To Use You,'* and *'Afterwhile.'* Our very own *Ronald King, Sr.* (now, Pastor Ronald King, shepherd of The Living Hope Christian Center, in Pennsauken, NJ) directed the choir along with Andrew Ford, Sr.

This recording was a tremendous success. Not only was this a success for us as a group, but it held Sweet Rain Records up as a credible corporation that would eventually reach many more heights beyond 1981. On August 18th of that same year, I gave birth to my *'recording baby.'* She weighed 6 lbs. 3 oz. We named her *'Sharita Joy.'* And yes, she sings like a sweet bird of paradise!

By 1983, the Alumni Choir would have recorded two (2) more albums and by January 12th of that year I would have had my last child, a son, who would later become a musical genius just like my brother, Byron, who appeared on all of the Wagner projects. We named this miracle child that crept up on us, Larry Jr., after his father. He was the last of our lot and God knew just how to do things, for we'd wanted a son and God had us wait until the very last child for him. I won't say that the best came last because all of our children are a joy. But, I will say that Larry Jr. was an unexpected blessing and continues to be even today! God truly gave me a song this time!

"More Philadelphia Stories"

It is obvious to me that Philadelphia breeds great groups and great choirs. Other cities may boast of having a few good groups, but only Philadelphia can pride itself as a cornucopia of great music and great personalities. In my lifetime I have witnessed legendary people perform such as: *Madame Ruth Irvin, Gladys Gordon, Gertrude Ward, Madame Bumpus, Morris Scott,* and *Ernest Davis.* These are but a few that I remember during my lifetime that helped shape how I think and how I perceive the music that I'm still singing today. And, the list goes on: *The Victory Choral Ensemble, The Brockington Ensemble, with Professor Irvin Brockington; The Savettes (with Elder Goldwire McClendon, of 2010's Sunday's Best fame); the Philadelphia Mass Choir,* and *the Wilmington Chester Mass Choir, under their founder, the late Rev. Ernest Davis.* One cannot forget *Jackie Verdell* and the *Davis Singers,* who also came out of the Philadelphia/Camden, NJ area; and let's not forget *Gabriel Hardeman and The Delegation.*

Another fact that the Philadelphia community can boast about is the impact that its *'church choirs'* have had on the music that affects how we worship and serve God. There is no doubt to the limitless influence that Apostolic and Holiness church choirs such as *B.M. Oakley Mass Choir; The Congregational Choir of the Rock of Ages Church; The Highway Church of Christ (under the directorship of Andrew and Steven Ford); the N.J. and P.A. United Holiness District Choir; Buddy Crosby and the Joy Night Choir; Beth El Sabbath Day Choirs (under Mother Daley's leadership),* ministered, along with scores of outstanding Baptist and Methodist church choirs in existence for over 50 years, all on one accord lifting songs of praises to the real 'King' of music, and ministering to the Body of Christ in ways that we're still reaping today as part of the rich heritage of Philadelphia's Gospel Music.

"Not Just Music"

Since 1983, I've gathered a few of my 'friends' *(Barbara Ward Farmer and Friends),* and recorded twice, with the *'Best of Wagner', and 'I Say, You Say.'* These projects were extremely important to me because I had a chance to minister through song in a way that I hadn't done before. I believe that purposefully, the LORD took me down a road of new beginnings, discoveries, development, preparation, and

I'm Still Singing

destiny, that would lead me to a world of *'only God'* and His true Divine nature to make me more and more like Him. I didn't know it at the time, but looking back, God was preparing me for something more than music. I found myself in a relationship with God that sharpened my senses, my hearing, my vision, my emotions, and my walk with Him. After the last chord was played and the last melody was sung, I still heard God speak to my soul leading me into a Christ-centered, Christ-inspired realm, where I found the yearning to lead others in a non-musical sense to hear the *'sound of God'* in their relationship with Him. My vision was now moving me to see God more than a B^b chord, but I was now endowed with a $C^\#$, Christ-induced love to seek and save those who are lost. Of course, the devil wanted me to lose my song of victory along the way, but God blocked it, and now I can look back and say, *"Surely The Great I Am will be there in the midst of your life's sharps and flats."* Now that's a song, hallelujah!

So, how do I see myself now, 60 years later? Well, I see myself as a favored vessel of God whose life is not just about music or musical apparatus, but my life now is impacted and inclusive with the ways of God and the Word of God. Remember that I told you about how in my early life I'd go to the Philadelphia Met where the different gospel performers would perform before hundreds of people? Well, I saw backstage, the *real* singers and musicians and how they *really* lived off-stage. As a child, I saw smoked filled hallways, bottles and cans of beer and other alcoholic beverages in the corners and on the tables, and I thought, **"Is this the real behavior of the gospel singer?"** Well, without judging them, I judged myself there and then, and I told myself that "*I would never be a hypocritical singer. I must be truthful. I must keep my body, God's temple, clean; and present my body a living sacrifice, holy, and acceptable before God which is my reasonable service.*" Having made this commitment long ago, after 60 years, I'm still singing!

Chapter Ten

"The National CLG Music Conference"

In the middle of the 1950's when my family and I moved to Penns Grove, N.J., in the worship services under the pastorate of Elder L.C. Williams, we were introduced to the House of God, which is the Church of The Living God, the Pillar and Ground of The Truth, Inc. For me, it wasn't simply a move of bodies and voices, but it was the move of a greater relationship of musical exposure that I was destined to learn and be trained in all areas of music, from the keyboard to the teaching of choral parts, directing, establishing the local, district, state, and later the national choirs throughout the Churches of The Living God, Inc. or CLG, as many of us call it. The Churches of The Living God is a fellowship of churches that got its roots in 1903 under the founding mother, Mother M.L. Tate. From Mother Tate, as she was affectionately called, our extension of CLG or *'Dominion'* came from one of her spiritual sons, Bishop Archibald Henry (A.H.) White. So, our now existing hundred and eighty some churches, national and international, extending to Africa, Jamaica, Haiti, and Trinidad, were all extensions of the *'White Dominion'* as we are frequently called. We are beneficiaries of the vision and work of the late Bishop A.H. White (I wanted you to know the history of my church affiliation because Bishop White performed my wedding on June 3, 1972 when he was a mere 93 years old, at his church, which was the Headquarters for the National Churches of The Living God, Inc. Bishop White would depart this life to his eternal reward nine years later in 1981 at the young age of 102 years old! He and CLG are a part of why I'm still singing!

Several years after Bishop A.H. White died, several more Bishops served in the office of Chief Prelate. However, in 1986, a young charismatic and well-loved man from Hartford, CT., Pastor Jesse J. White, Sr., (a nephew of Bishop A.H. White) was chosen to be the Presiding Prelate of the National Churches of The Living God. He would serve for more than 20 years – from 1986 to 2008.

It was under the leadership of Bishop Jesse J. White, that a young man from Columbus, Ohio, who came from a long line of singers and preachers would become our National Minister of Music for the entire organization. His name was Elder Roger Hairston, Sr. He was a highly anointed singer, songwriter, prophet, and preacher who transformed and raised CLG's music to another level.

By this time, I had recorded several albums and had gained popularity throughout the country and had even started to travel internationally. Since CLG knew me as a singer working under the tutelage of some of its musical pioneers of excellence, such as: the late Professor Edward G. Robinson, of Detroit, MI., Jerry and Bishop-elect Benjamin Drone, from Akron, OH, Bishop Leila Jenkins, from Philadelphia, PA., and William "Junior Marshall, from Springfield, MA., I was elected to be Elder Hairston's assistant and functioned in that capacity for many years.

By the year 2000, Elder Hairston was consecrated to the Bishopric. Prior to this elevation however, in 1989, he and I founded CLG's conference for music which became the National CLG Music Conference. We had our very first meeting in Harrisburg, PA., where the late Apostle Patricia Jones served as our Host Pastor and supervisor until her death. Still functioning today, the Music Conference was formed to build up the music ministries throughout the country and to enhance the departments in the areas of musicianship, directing, choir decorum, understanding true praise and worship, and vocal techniques, to name a few.

This conference allowed me to establish long lasting relationships with the country's greatest conveyors of the sound of God through music to the world. Some of the people I was blessed to work with were the Herndons, from Harrisburg, PA, Pastor Ramona Kinard and family, of York, PA., the late Troy Hopkins, also of York, PA., Rev. Jamar Jones, of Philadelphia, PA, (who now serves at the Potter's House in Dallas, TX); Darrell Williams, Donte Thompson, James Penn, Damien, Melody Sherman-Tate, Will Suddeth, and Antoine Walker, of Akron, OH; Professor Gary Lewis, Anthony McMullen, and Jimmy Parker, from Cleveland, OH; Elder Kelvin Ransey and his family, from Toleho, OH (now Bishop Ransey, residing in Tupelo, MS; Chiquita (Chi Chi) Nabors, of Detroit, MI; my brother and sister – Byron Ward and Carole Ellerbe, of Phila., PA and Pennsauken, NJ respectively; Doug Majors, of Leesburg, FL; Latrice Glenn, of Orlando, FL; Curtis Andrews, of Camden, NJ (now a Harrisburg, PA resident); the late Elder Jimmy McClain, of Chicago, IL; Margaret Estelle (my successor as the current National Minister of Music for CLG) of Hartford, CT; J.C. and Betty Beene, of Tupelo, MS; George "Buddy" Parks, Bro. Mario, Bro. Quadris, and Bro. Genaris, all from MS; and the organizers and directors from Buchtel and Firestone High Schools in Akron, OH.

It was the support of my mother, Bishop Lillian Ward (Camden, NJ), the late Bishop David Drone, of Akron, OH, and the late Apostle Patricia Jones, who supported our earlier efforts that will always be imprinted in my mind. Apostle Gus Sullivan, and Bishop William Jones, and his members were also supportive to us in the beginning stages of the conference.

In 1993, the National Music Conference singers and musicians recorded their first album in Columbus, OH. The music was outstanding and my partner, Bishop Hairston was the producer of the project (we are still singing some of those songs today). The singers, musicians, and directors comprising CLG's Mass Choir learned an album full of songs in 2½ days. I shall never forget the favor of the LORD during that recording. In 1996, the CLG Mass Choir recorded again, during the National Youth Congress, which was held in Harrisburg, PA that year. It was here that the LORD blessed me to produce my first album with the CLG Mass Choir.

Now, in 2014, although I'm no longer the National Minister of Music for CLG, I have been appointed as the Liaison Bishop for the National Music Ministry for the National Churches of the Living God. I believe I was chosen to this post because of my over 25 years of service to this auxiliary at my home church and for the national organization of CLG.

In memoriam, I want to thank God for Apostle Pat Jones, of Harrisburg, PA; Brother James Knight, of Connecticut; Pastor Jimmy McClain, of Chicago, IL; Pastor Troy Hopkins, of York, PA; and Brother Eric Sherman, Jr., of Toledo, OH, who served in the CLG Music Conference and gave their lives to the service of the LORD.

It is also fitting to acknowledge that before there was a music conference there were those who pioneered in the music of CLG, who blessed us and made an impact on our music throughout our churches: the late Professor Edward G. Robinson, the late Bishop David Drone, his brothers Jerry and Benjamin Drone, Bishop Joseph White, Attorney Garnita Selby, William Marshall, Cindy Barber, Elder Ruth Denison, and the Jenkins Family, of Philadelphia, PA.

CHAPTER ELEVEN

"From Spiritual Ministry to Spiritual Leader"

I'm still singing about keeping my body holy before God. I'm still singing about living a sanctified and satisfied life for God. I'm still singing that to the uttermost – Jesus Saves! I'm still singing that Jesus can and will heal you, set you free, and deliver you from whatever has you bound. I'm still singing that "a charge to keep I have, and a God to glorify."

The music that God has enriched me to experience has taken me to places that I could only dream of going. Besides traveling extensively throughout the United States, I have ministered in music and Word in Europe, Asia, and Africa.

I have been blessed to have four (4) children: *Larita, Benita, Sharita Joy, and Larry, Jr.* I have two (2) beautiful extended children by way of marriage – my daughter-in-law, Sabrina (Larry, Jr.), and son-in-law Thorn (Sharita Joy). I have five (5) grandchildren whom I adore, and lots of talented nieces, nephews, and cousins. Of my children, Benita is a gospel recording artist, and Larry Jr., a producer, respectively. Hallelujah, I'm blessed to have my seed blessed too!

And of course, not many women at my age who are busy in ministry whether in song or in the public speaking ministry as Pastor or Bishop can say that they are happily married and satisfied with the *'same man'* for over 41 years. *Since the age of fifteen, I have loved and been faithful to the same man (he was 16), extremely handsome and gorgeous, 'Lawrence', or 'Larry' as we sometimes call him, Farmer; the father of my four (4) children, my lover, and best earthly friend.* The success of our relationship is simple. It's been God-ordained, God-sanctioned, and God-driven. We have been friends for 43 years. As my lover, my husband, my boyfriend, my trumpet player and Head Trustee of my church, God has truly anointed Larry to keep me singing, hallelujah!

I have experienced a beautiful epoch of teaching for over 25 years in the public schools of Pennsylvania (PA) and New Jersey (NJ) before retiring to enter into full-time ministry. I have been blessed to carry God's word for over 37 years, including the privilege to serve as pastor of the Faith Tabernacle Church in Camden, N.J., for fifteen years, the church that my mother founded and pastored for over 19 years during my years of ministering. I have had only one dark day that I can recall that affected me and still leaves a void in my life. That is the day that my daddy died, March 24, 2005. *Elder Edward Ward, Sr., was something to sing about!* He was a hard worker and a humble man, who retired after 30 years of service at the Campbell Soup Company, in Camden, NJ. He had an exemplary work ethic that colored every facet of his life. Dad's humility, integrity, tenacity and passion for God, family, and the things of God could be seen in everything that he did. His work ethic was evident in the church as well, where he served without reservation, resentment or intimidation as the Assistant Pastor to my mother, who was now a Bishop in the Churches of The Living God, under the leadership of Bishop A. H. White, who was the Presiding Prelate at the time. For over 25 years my father could be found praising God at Faith Tabernacle Church on any given Sunday, while yet taking out the trash, fixing a door, or in the kitchen cooking one of his most delicious meals for the 'Bishop' or for anyone who might be at the church during the week. He was the same way at home, too. It was rare for Daddy to be found doing absolutely nothing. He enjoyed reading, and although he lacked a formal education, he read a lot and was more than sufficiently self-taught. He had a thirst for knowledge and enjoyed discussing things he'd learned, and he took pleasure in sharing his 'experiments' or special recipes with virtually anyone. He relished sharing because these 'experiments' always more than excelled at passing the taster's test. Also, Daddy was ahead of his time. He talked much about natural remedies and the benefits of them long before they became popularized. My dad's humble, quiet demeanor did not leave him lacking, either. He garnered the love, admiration, and respect of anyone he encountered. His spirit of praise and worship was contagious, as well as his gift of hospitality. For, although he was the Assistant Pastor, husband of the pastor, and father of the well-known Evangelist Barbara Ward Farmer, he could still be found alone at the church at almost any hour, adorned in an apron, cleaning, sweeping, and cooking, repairing something – he'd do whatever needed to be done at the church and around the house too. He was the essence of a godly, manly support to a woman of God in leadership, and a shining example to his sons and daughters of what a real man of God is. So much of what my mother was able to accomplish in ministry, and what my siblings and I have been able to accomplish both in and out of the church setting can be attributed to this quiet, humble, inquisitive and courageous man. Together, my parents labored in the church in Camden, NJ, although they lived in Philadelphia, PA. They loved the LORD and they loved each other and were married for 55 years.

    The night of my father's death, I was preaching at Apostle Bruce Lester's church, in Camden, N.J. God did not give me a warning, but He did give me a sign that the end was near. Someone had called my husband to tell me to come quickly to the hospital. So, after service, without letting me know that my family was already called and had gathered at the hospital, when I got in the car my husband drove about four blocks and then said, "Barbara, we have to go to the hospital now." I asked him, "Why?" He then told me that my dad didn't make it. My friends, when Larry told me that, it seemed as if the music suddenly stopped, the song was over and the band could no longer just play on.

By the time we reached the hospital I was completely numb and tone deaf for the first time in my life. But God is so faithful! When I thought that I could never hear the music anymore, or that I could never sing in harmony again, God truly gave me another reason to hear the sweet sounds of His voice and He put another song in my heart! He gave the instrument of my heart a Divine tune-up! Hallelujah!!! I don't know just how or when God did it, but He lifted me *and* my family up and He is still comforting us from our great loss. It's truly amazing to me how only God can keep a melody in your heart that will never change keys or resonance even in the midst of loss and grief. I can truly say that despite circumstance, only in Christ can the song of peace, joy, and love keep playing synergistically to comfort you when you need it the most.

There are so many songs that have kept me singing all of these years, from *'Walk With Me, LORD,' 'I Don't Know Why Jesus Loves Me,' 'Afterwhile It Will All Be Over,' 'Wait On The LORD,'* and *'I Have Never Seen The Righteous Forsaken!'* But, it is Myrna Summers' song from the 70's that has been my heart source, the rhythms and beats of my life: <u>*"God gave me a song, that the angels cannot sing..."*</u>

It was also in the 1960's and 1970's that the music of Andre Couch inspired me to sing outside of my race. It was Andre Crouch who showed me that true Gospel music is not confined to the African American race, but that the song of Christ is to every creature around the world. Andre's songs like, "Soon and Very Soon," "Take Me Back," "To God Be The Glory," and one of my favorites, "Jesus Is LORD," became songs that made me sing because they all talked about the reason, the rhyme, and the rationale of Jesus and why He's worthy to be praised. I didn't know it then, but I now know that a song without Jesus is a song without a melody – a rhythm without a beat – a sound that's impossible to be heard.

How can I say it any other way? After all that I've been through, after all that I have experienced, after all the losses and gains in my life, I haven't stopped praising my God and my LORD. I haven't stopped listening to His voice. I haven't stopped giving and believing. I haven't stopped serving and studying His Word. I haven't stopped loving God and His people more than my own life. I'm so glad to report to all that I meet that after 60 years of hearing the 'sound of God,' *"I'm Still Singing!"*

"From Spiritual Minstrel To Spiritual Leader"

As long as I can remember, all I ever wanted to do was to sing and evangelize while singing. But after many words of prophesy and with the laying on of hands by the Presiding Bishop and Elders of the church, I submitted myself to the will of God and began to pastor His flock at the same church that I sang and grew up in, in Camden, N.J. So, in 1995, Faith Tabernacle, CLG became my assignment, although I'd fought the decision to pastor Faith for many years, not knowing that my mother (who had herself long since been elevated and was now my Bishop), had felt the leading of the LORD to transfer the Mosaic call onto me, the Joshua of 1995. I said "yes" and yielded to God's will in January of that same year.

It seemed strange when people began calling me *'Pastor Farmer'* instead of the constant call and presentation of *Evangelist Barbara Ward Farmer* that I'd grown so accustomed to over the years, especially while on the road singing with the Wagner Alumni Choir, and before that the tag name of 'Little Miss Barbara Ann Ward. All in all, these felt like major transformations that marked periods of my life, both spiritually and naturally. This was a period in which my life as a singer showed signs of similarity with my life now as a pastor. First of all, I had developed the same love for my members as I had for the souls in the audiences at the various churches and auditoriums I encountered and ministered to across America. Second, I wanted to see a change in the hope, belief, thoughts and behavior of the parishioners, just as I'd wanted to see in the crowds that I sang to who gathered at Wagner Jr. High, Wagner Alumni Choir and Wagner Friends' concerts. It is pointless to perform but not minister. And, I wanted to truly bless people so they could bless God, so that He would be glorified with each and every concert and appearance, and that they each went beyond performance into ministry. Accordingly, I discovered that God developed this heart in me through music so that my approach to pastoring would require the same kind of heart for Him and His sheep – a heart to ultimately lead them to Him. Additionally, I still had a desire for excellence in the form of congregational praise and worship and choral music just as I stressed excellence in live performances on the road.

Again, although I gave up my public performances with the Wagner Alumni Choir a year or two after I began to pastor, I still kept my desire to always have good music around me. Choir members such as Pastors Ronald King and Overseer Wendell Miller (both formerly my students at Wagner Jr. High), and musicians Pastor Jared Crawford (my bass player), and Pastor Lavel Johnson (my drummer); Jamar Jones (keyboards and organist), who now serves on the musical staff of Bishop T.D. Jakes of Dallas, TX.; and Elder Rodney Green of Pennsauken, NJ (organist), were playing at the church during my early years as Pastor. They were a tremendous blessing, skilled in bringing good music to the church. Elder Carole Ellerbe, my baby sister, who sang on all of Wagner's albums, became our unofficial Minister of Music, directing and orchestrating the music program at the church after former director and chief songwriter, Ronald King,

I'm Still Singing

left in preparation to enter into pastoral ministry, initiating his own church in New Jersey, with his lovely wife, Angie.

God truly moves and operates in mysterious ways. Although my brother Byron was the *'Professor of Wagner's music,'* by 2002 we had been blessed with talents such as Ronald King, Jamar Jones, Rodney Green, Isaac Phillips, Keith Simpson, and my nephews Cory Stallworth and Andre Ward, and my daughter-in-law, Sabrina (Larry, Jr) blessed Faith Tabernacle with their gifts and talents for many years. But then God did something – He raised up one who was my very own – my one and only son, Larry Jr., to be the church organist, and my second daughter, Benita, to become our Minister of Music, who'd direct and coordinate the musical program in our church. She remains in that capacity even to this day as of this writing. Thus, God kept me singing musically through Benita and Larry Jr. Benita has of this writing recorded two (2) complete albums or CD's (as they say in the 21st century) and a single, appeared on projects with the noteworthy, anointed, Maurette Brown Clark, and appeared on TBN ministering the Word in song; while Larry Jr. has produced his big sis's last project and written various musical pieces eventually to be televised in the near future. He has also traveled throughout the U.S. and abroad playing for Camden's own, Ty Tribbett and Greater Anointing. Larry has also written and produced his own musical and video production, and is himself in the process of writing a book, all under the pen name of "Black Surfer." Appropriately, the name "Black Surfer" represents the power of God through visual and audio. [Look for a Black Surfer Production in your area real soon!].

When David the King declared in Psalm 36, that he once was young and was now old and had never seen the righteous forsaken or his seed begging bread, I believe he prophetically saw me in 2010. When one sings as a songwriter brilliantly put it, *'because he is happy, free, and is watched over like the sparrow that flies freely,'* he has a testimony of varied life experiences and survival. *Truly, the afflictions of the righteous are many, but the LORD delivers them from them all!* Listen to my testimony: **"I am happy."** I'm happy because after all of these years, I'm still saved, delivered, and healed. I've slipped, but I kept on standing. I've cried, but kept my smile. I've been pushed off key, but God gave me a tune-up, hallelujah, when His blood kept covering me! **I'm still singing because I'm free.** I'm free because the Son said so!

After all of these years, many solos later, many groups and choirs later, many concerts later, I'm free to love God all I want to. I'm free from condemnation and guilt. But most of all, **I'm free to be me** – *the me* that nobody wants, *the me* that the builders rejected, *the me* that Christ said I'm worth dying for, *the me* that has value and worth."

Many have stopped or refused to sing anymore because they; **a)** lost their voice or their way; **b)** forgot how to sing or what to sing; **c)** would rather cry, moan, complain, or fight then to remain a nonconformist of the ways of God. But if anyone asks you, *"What is Barbara Ward Farmer doing now?",* you may tell them that she is still in church, still a mother, wife, sister, grandmother, daughter, aunt, mother-in-law, pastor, teacher, director, community activist; and, still saved, sanctified, and filled with the Holy Ghost. She is still standing, encouraging, exhorting and equipping the believers, evangelizing the world and holding on to the Word of God. But, most of all, tell everyone who knows me and those who have never heard of me or any of my life's achievements, that after all of these 60 years, through natural and supernatural growing pains of joys and sorrows, ups and downs, twists and turns, tests and trials, losses and gains, victories and seeming defeats – *I'm still singing the praises of my LORD, Savior, and King!* Through it all I've grown in every way. I've simply learned all the more to trust in Jesus, and to trust in God. You see, the melody of Christ brought harmony to my life that has grown clearer to my hearing, thus more harmonious over the years. I hear the harmony of Christ in my heart clearer as I continue to grow in Him. As the harmony continues, so must I. That's why I'm still singing. Truly, He has used *'life'* to exemplify His word to me. **All things have worked together for my good. All things!** Hallelujah! That is why whatever storm comes, as well as whatever joy arises, I know that if I could sing through yesterday, I can sing through today. If I can sing *after* yesterday, I can sing *after* whatever is happening today. My God is the same yesterday, today, and forevermore. Therefore, what He did for me yesterday, He'll do today. Even more! I teach my people that *'you don't need a miracle; all you need is a memory!'* God has *'performed'* His word in my life as I have *'performed'* His word in song. So, I must continue to sing for Him. You see, He is an eternal God, and He's given me an *eternal song.* And even beyond today, when you have heard word of this *'psalmist soldier'* going home to meet the LORD, you can yet surely testify for me what I have testified to you of in this book today in the here and now, that beyond the clouds into the heavens, gathered 'round the throne of my Father, Savior and LORD, I have taken my place with a flock of angels and am doing there for eternity what God purposed and equipped me to do, even here on earth. *To sing of His wondrous works; His wondrous praise; His wondrous attributes, character, and His wondrous Name. He is proven worthy now and forevermore, and that is why –* **I'm Still Singing!!!**

I'm still singing
I have something to sing about;
I'm still singing
Watch me move, dance, and shout

I'm still singing
I have a song that you have not heard yet;
I'm still singing
I have known many people that even you have never met

Bishop Dr. Barbara Ward Farmer

I'm still singing
About songs of hope and songs to teach;
I'm still singing,
Singing to everyone that I hope to reach

I'm still singing
Through my losses and the battles that I've won;
I'm still singing
Now my doubts and fears are all gone

I'm still singing
Although the music may have stopped ringing
If anybody asks whatever happened to me;

Encourage them with these words of hope

She kept on, she kept on into the heavenlies
Where she's still singing!

Chapter Twelve

"International Traveler"

God has beautiful ways of showing us special favor from time to time. Subsequent to my recording days with the Wagner Alumni Choir, news about this group from Philadelphia reached deep, far, and wide across the country. In the late 1980's to early 1990's the choir and I sang at the very popular Black Gospel College Festival that was held every year in Atlanta, GA at the Peach Tree Hotel. It was later held at the Omni Hotel and Conference Center in Atlanta during the Thanksgiving Day weekend. I can't recall the exact year, but we were invited to perform even though we were not a college choir. But, one of the coordinators of the event was our producer, Andrew Ford, Jr. (now Bishop Andrew Ford, of Phila., PA) who arranged for us to be placed on the schedule to sing. We were scheduled for a Thursday night and we were excited and full of anticipation. We fasted, prayed, and prepared, surrendering our gifts to the LORD. And, on the night that we were scheduled to sing, the place was packed with choirs from everywhere! It was intimidating to a degree, and we found ourselves sitting in our robes nervously waiting to be called on. Well, by 9:20pm we were still waiting. At 11:30pm, we were still waiting. By 12am, and after a third of the crowd had left – they finally called us to the stage. By then, our nervousness had run its course and we weren't in the least upset about the lateness of our performance for we had traveled too far from Philly to Atlanta to imagine not having the opportunity to sing at all. That would have been disappointing. Besides, believe it or not, we were just 'glad to be in the number' of those called on, so we were still excited!

Well, my friends, when we climbed onto that massive stage with our 5-piece rhythm section, 5-piece horn section, and this vibrant, anointed group of young people who were ready to minister in song regardless of the lateness of the hour, the LORD met us there, anointed us to sing as never before, and Shekinah glory came down in that place at midnight! After we left the stage, the Omni Hotel and Conference Center was still filled with the presence of the LORD. Clearly God had done something and was doing something even more. For, word travelled across Atlanta that a "Holy-Ghost filled, sanctified-looking choir had *brought the house down* at midnight at the Omni."

Now, when you go to these type of musical college conferences, you get to perform once and that's it. However, the LORD favored us so, that we were asked to return the next night, this time to *'open'* for this prestigious annual event. And, the LORD met us there again the second night!

I love sharing this experience because it is evidence of God's power and pleasure in opening doors for us. His *'exceedingly, abundantly, above all that we ask or think'* power was surely demonstrated here with me and this group of young people. For, even though we didn't know it at the time, it would be this experience along with our first recording that would open city doors wide for us to enter and sing the gospel in cities throughout the U.S.A., and especially in the state of Florida. For the next 4 to 5 years after the Atlanta, GA experience, we literally *stayed* in Florida, travelling from Jacksonville to Miami, a span of 900+ miles at 13+ hours of travel time on the road. We either toured or I was asked to do workshops it seemed everywhere.

I'm Still Singing

I traveled to Texas, Louisiana, Massachusetts, Ohio, Michigan, and various places throughout New Jersey, Pennsylvania, and Delaware.

During the early 1990's, one of our CLG young men was serving in the military in Germany and he invited me and a team of musicians and singers to come to Germany to minister. What an experience this would turn out to be! Clearly, this was divinely arranged, for God gave me favor to share the music of Christ Jesus with the United States Air Force in Germany. I would be invited back another year and blessed with the same warm spirit that had greeted me and my team the first time we visited there.

A few years later, the LORD again favored me to travel – this time to Asia, then Europe, and finally Africa. Each time that I went to these places, I taught hundreds of people both native and military, and souls received the LORD. In all, I went to Germany-twice, Japan-3times, Korea-once, Italy-once, and Lagos, Nigeria for 7-9 days preaching and teaching the Gospel of Jesus Christ.

In the early 2000's, I traveled to Puerto Rico to preach twice, and to the Bahamas to conduct a 3-day crusade. Traveling to international places was a tremendous blessing to me because I not only had the opportunity to exercise my teaching and preaching skills on people who were unfamiliar with me as a singer or a pastor, but I truly felt that I was completing 'The Great Commission' of Matthew 28:19-20, **"*Therefore go and make disciples of all nations, baptizing them in the name of the Father and of the Son and of the Holy Spirit, and teaching them to obey everything I have commanded you. And surely I am with you always, to the very end of the age.*"**

The people of these lands learned and sang the following 'Wagner' songs:

'Never Seen The Righteous Forsaken'   *(Ronald King, Sr.)*
'Refuge For My Soul'   *(Ronald King, Sr.)*

'99½ Won't Do'	*(Ronald King, Sr.)*
'Wait On The LORD'	*(Barbara Ward Farmer)*
'He Wants To Use You'	*(Barbara Ward Farmer)*
'Never Stop Praising Him'	*(Barbara Ward Farmer)*
'I Will Extol Thee'	*(Barbara Ward Farmer)*
'The Windows of Heaven'	*(Barbara Ward Farmer)*
'Lift Him Up'	*(Barbara Ward Farmer)*
'People Get Ready'	*(Barbara Ward Farmer)*
'Valley Praise'	*(Isaac Phillips)*

I taught the various choirs these songs, and my brother, Byron Ward, worked with the military bands in Germany and Japan. When I went to Korea, Jamar Jones accompanied me and worked with the musicians there. And in 2006, when I went to Italy and again to Japan, I was blessed to have my son, Larry Jr., work with the musicians and my sister, Carole, assisted with the voices.

I will always remember my international travel as a series of unique experiences through which God demonstrated the awesomeness of His power and the truth of His word to me. He is my Blessed Assurance, just as The Psalmist purports in Psalm 121:5-8, *"The LORD is thy keeper: the LORD is thy shade upon thy right hand. The sun shall not smite thee by day, nor the moon by night. The LORD shall preserve thee from all evil: He shall preserve thy soul. The LORD shall preserve thy going out and thy coming in from this time forth, and even forevermore!"*

Chapter Thirteen

"I'm Still Singing!"

According to the Wikipedia's definition of 'singing' assessed on April 1, 2014, *"singing is the act of producing musical sounds with the voice and augments regular speech by the use of both tonality and rhythm. One who sings is called a singer or vocalist. Singers perform music (arias, recitatives, songs, etc.), that can be sung either with or without the accompaniment of musical instruments. Singing is often done in a group of other musicians, such as in a choir of singers with different voice ranges, or in an ensemble (a group smaller than a choir) with instrumentalists such as a rock group or baroque ensemble."*

In the former eleven chapters of this book, it has been my intention to share with you my life of music as a singer, from my birth until the present. And as I ponder my life, now at age 63, it's clear that I've sung in churches, arenas, auditoriums, stadiums and outdoor events, theatres, universities and colleges, and various places within the United States and countries spanning four continents of the world. But, I realize something about myself all of these years. I realize that I've been singing even when I wasn't performing. I gave my voice to those issues that as a believer, preacher, and teacher, God wanted me to *'make known His deeds among the people.'* Every time I let my light come through, every time I stood on principles representing Jesus Christ, I was singing.

Whenever I performed I realize that this was my public demonstration of a skill and gift that God had given to me. This was an expression of music rehearsed, practiced and learned to reflect what I now know had to be heard because of the demand for an 'artist.' However, I realize that my singing changed when Christ came into my life at the tender young age of 11 years old.

Now, the sound of music for me is the *sound of God* 'walking' within me. It gave me purpose. Every time I obeyed the voice of God, it changed my voice to evolve into the right pitch, volume, tone, and 'beat of God.'

Every song, whether it's a good song should have three things: *a message, meaning, and a purpose.* Some artists write their own songs or arrange their own compositions with worldwide appeal, style, and flavor. Gospel singers should understand however, that when you sing, it shouldn't be about what people want but about what they need. And, the world needs to be saved. The world needs to be healed. The world needs to be delivered!

Now, at 63 years of age, I don't perform anymore but I'm still singing! How? When? Why? When I preach and teach now, I'm singing the message that Jesus is still the answer, and that He died so that we might live! Yes, I'm still singing! When I preach and teach today, my message has meaning. Christ is worthy to be embraced as one's LORD, Savior, and King. My singing today reveals that according to a Corinthians 5:17, *"If any man be in Christ, he is a new creature; old things are passed away; behold all things are become new."* The meaning of a life in Christ means change for the better and fulfillment. I still go around the cities of Camden, NJ, Philadelphia, PA and the Greater Delaware Valley area, or wherever the LORD sends me or gives me the opportunity to still sing in the key of A^b – *acknowledge that you need a Savior.* Then I switch to ***B*** natural – believe on the LORD Jesus Christ and you shall be saved. But my favorite is **C major** – *no sharps or flats – confess with your mouth Jesus as LORD*. Finally, my purpose in singing in the keys of **F, D, G, and E**, are as follows:

- F = faithful is our God
- D = deliverance for all
- G = great is the power of God
- E = Everlasting life is given to all who believe and receive Christ as Savior.

What King David recorded in Psalm 101:1-4a sums up why I'm still singing: *"I will sing of mercy and judgment: unto Thee O LORD, will I sing. I will behave myself wisely in a perfect way. O when wilt thou come with me? I will walk within my house with a perfect heart. I will set no wicked thing before mine eyes: I hate the work of them that turn aside; it shall not cleave to me. A forward heart shall depart from me."*

So, why am I still singing and living for God even though I no longer *'perform'* publicly? The answer is found in Psalm 92:12-15 – *"The righteous shall flourish like the palm tree: he shall grow like a cedar in Lebanon. Those that be planted in the House of the LORD shall flourish in the courts of our God. They shall still bring forth fruit in old age; they shall be fat and flourishing; to shew that the LORD is upright: He is my rock and there is no unrighteousness in Him."*

CHAPTER FOURTEEN

"Something To Sing About: A Chronological Scope of My Lifetime Achievements"

1954	Sang publicly for the first time, in Philadelphia, PA, at age 4
1962	Sang as soloist throughout East Coast
1961	Won a contract to record Received Baptism of the Holy Ghost
	Recorded first and only '45' (single) in New York City
1965	Met Larry Farmer (my husband)
1966	Recorded with the National Church (Churches of The Living God) in Harrisburg, PA.
1967-68	Membership in the prestigious Philadelphia All City High Schools Choir; Performed at the Academy of Music and The Spectrum, with the Philadelphia All City High School Choir in concert with the Philadelphia All City High School Orchestra
	June '68 – graduated from South Philadelphia High School with honors and as Senior Class President.

1969   *January* – Enrolled freshman year at West Chester State College (now West Chester State University) in West Chester, PA.
Joined my mother in moving from National Temple CLG, in Penns Grove, N.J., to start Faith Tabernacle CLG, in Camden, N.J.

1970   Started the first Gospel Choir at West Chester State College.

1972   *May* – Graduated from West Chester College with a Baccalaureate degree (B.S.) in Spanish Education
June 3 – married teenage sweetheart Larry Farmer
September – Preached initial sermon at Faith Tabernacle Church, Began teaching in Philadelphia, PA, at Wagner Jr. High School
December – Granted permission by the principal of Wagner Jr. High School to form a school choir. Rehearsal set for 8 a.m., in the school auditorium. Over 50 students showed up for our very first rehearsal.

1973   *December 8th* – gave birth to first child, a daughter *'Larita'*

1975   *September 26th* – gave birth to second child, daughter *'Benita'*

1978   Ordained as an Elder in the church

1978-79   Wagner Alumni Choir of Philadelphia is formed in Philly's West Oak Lane section at the old Second Macedonia Baptist Church…

1980   *September* – Began teaching ESL (English As A Second Language) to adult students in NJ

1981   *June 6th* – Wagner records first album in Philadelphia, PA. I am seven (7) months pregnant at the time.
August 18th – gave birth to third child, daughter, *'Sharita Joy'*

I'm Still Singing

1983	*January 12th* – gave birth to fourth and last child, a son, *'Larry Jr.'*
1994	Recorded with Wagner Alumni Choir and Friends in four projects: *'Refuge For My Soul,' 'Peace In Heaven,' 'I Say You Say,'* and *'The Best of Wagner'*
1986	*April* – Began teaching ESL (English As A Second Language) to Hispanic bilingual children in Camden, NJ
1986-94	Traveled to Germany, Japan, and Korea, conducting musical workshops
1988 -	Joined the Administrative Branch of the National Churches of The Living
2010	God's Music Ministry, Co-founding the National CLG Music Conference with Bishop Roger Hairston of Columbus, OH, and serving initially as the National Assistant Minister of Music, then later as the National Minister of Music for the National Churches of The Living God.
1995	*January* – Installed as Pastor of Faith Tabernacle Church in Camden, NJ
	June – Retired from teaching in the Public School System after 25 years.
1998	*April* – With husband, Larry Farmer, established the LaBar Day Care, Inc., at the Faith Tabernacle Church, CLG.
2000	Joined forces with Community Advocates and clergy in the City of Camden.
2003	Son Larry and daughter Benita begin to display their musical artistries.
2005	*September* – traveled to Lagos, Nigeria for ministry at the Redeemed Church; one of, if not the largest Christian organization in Nigeria

2006	Purchased an additional building in Camden, NJ, on Chestnut Street. This would be the location for Early Childcare Education, and would be named after my parents who assisted in financing the completion of this project. Thus, *'The Ward Center For Children.'*
	October – traveled to Italy with son, Larry Jr., for music workshop. He was the picture of awesomeness, reminding me of my gifted brother, his Uncle Byron, who accompanied me on my European and Asian tours (1986-94)
2008	*October 31st* – consecrated to the office of Bishop in the Churches of The Living God, in Greensboro, North Carolina.
2010	*March* – Received *Director of the Year Award* Recipient of the *Dream Keeper Award*, Camden, NJ – Community Activist Group, Camden, NJ
2011	*November*–Nominated, honored, and selected as an African American Clergy Woman of Distinction by the Alpha Phi Alpha Chapter of NJ
2014	*April* – received honorary Doctorate Degree from St. Thomas Christian University, in Jacksonville, FL.

Still Singing About The Glory of God!!!

FACTS

Birth – 1950
Day – 9/5 (Monday)
Weather – nice, sunny morning
Atmosphere – great, a girl!
Family's Reaction – maternal grandmother predicted I'd be a singer mother sang to me and I sang back to her
Toddler's Characteristics / Personality – mischievous
Earliest Childhood Memories – home: 2624 Ellsworth St., South Philadelphia; the house, neighborhood, school, teachers, and church

Major Childhood Performances –

- ***First Performance – 4 years of age****...Song – 'I Want Jesus To Walk With Me'*
- ***At 5 yrs. old****, was part of the line-up at the 'Clara Ward and The Ward Singers'*
- *Anniversary at the Arena,* a large edifice in Phila., PA, It was an historical event., for it was the first time that a gospel event took place there...
- **My *first television performance at age 8 yrs. old.*** Appeared on Philadelphia's popular ABC-TV children's program, 'The Chief Halftown Show,' which featured local talents of various art forms from in and around the Greater Philadelphia area. I sang a gospel song because that was the 'music' that was in me. Appeared on the show three times from 1958-1963.
- ***First recording at age 11:*** won recording contract with Revelations Records, NYC, w/Becky Carlton on the organ; Composer/Songwriter was Evangelist Rosie Wallace Brown;

Songs were – *"What Do You Think About Jesus?"* and *"By The Grace of God"*

<u>Age 11 years</u> – received Holy Ghost

- *Contemporary Child Gospel Artists–* Little Larry Hood, Sandra Peyton, Beck Brothers, Sapp Sisters
- *Early Accompanists and Influences* – Jimmy Smith, Jimmy Washington, Bernard Chandler;
- 50's and 60's at the Philadelphia Met – Quartet Groups, Women's Groups, such as the late great Rudolph Lewis, Gospel Clefs, Newberry Singers, and the Thompson Sisters

Early Radio Years (Live – age 7 or 8) through the 1980's: These are the DJ's who played my music at varying times over a span of years, thus having an impact on my life and music over three decades, from the 1950's to the 1980's.

Gospel (WHAT)	**Secular (WDAS)**
Mary Dee (early)	Georgie Woods (early)
Bonnie Dee (later)	Kaye Williams (early)
Mary Mason (early)	
Walter Stewart (later)	
Lenwood Heath (later)	
Louise Williams (WDAS)	

The Church Scene – *Apostolic/ Holiness Influences*

National – Dr. Mattie Moss Clark
Conference Songs – Bibleway "Stay With God"
Reverend James Cleveland

Late 60's, Northern California Choir – Edwin and Walter Hawkins, and Tramaine Davis

The Philadelphia Connection (and surrounding areas) –Gertrude and Clara Ward

Victory Chorale Ensemble

Brockington Ensemble

Savettes

Philadelphia Mass Choir

Wilmington-Chester Mass Choir

The Church Scene#2 –

Local – Rock of Ages, Camden, NJ

B.M. Oakley Mass Choir

Several Baptist Churches - Cornerstone, Oak Grove, Monumental, and Zion Hill, etc.

Highway Church of Christ - Andrew and Stephen Ford

United Holiness Church N.J./P.A. District Choir

Bethel Sabbath Day Keeper Organization (under Mother Daley)

Ranges Temple, Chester, PA

National Temple Church of The Living God

Church of The Living God, Egg Harbor, NJ

Buddy Crosby and the Joy Night Choirs

Classical Influence and Musical Ear Development – Benson Elementary Audenreid Jr. High Schools (both schools in South Philadelphia)

Epilogue

As of this writing, I am now 63 years old. I can truly say what the Gospel singing group, The Winans popularized, *"I've been kept all this time, and I still have a mind to go on."* For, God has truly been good to me and has indeed shown me favor in all that I've done, spoken, and placed in my heart to do. My music has taken me to places that I could have only dreamed about. And, blessedly, I have met various people from different countries, continents, and towns throughout the United States.

I have written songs in English and in Spanish as well. Koreans, Japanese, Italians, Germans, and Nigerians have sung many of my English-based songs. I have taught preschoolers, elementary, middle school, high school and college students. I have taught various gospel choirs, Women's and Men's choirs, and even Senior Citizen's groups. I've shared the Gospel in song to various communities in the Pennsylvania, New Jersey, and Delaware Tri-State area. God has favored me to impact the world with the sound of gospel music with White, Black, Asian, and Latino cultures fulfilling what the Great Commission that Christ mandated believers in Matthews 28:19-20, *"Go ye therefore, and teach all nations, baptizing them in the name of the Father, and the Son, and the Holy Ghost: Teaching them to observe all things whatsoever I have commanded you; and, lo I am with you always, even unto the end of the world. Amen."*

Just looking at this mandate makes me reflect over the many years that God has preserved me to help preserve others; blessed me, so that I can be a blessing to others; kept me so I can be a symbol to others that the supernatural power of an Almighty God can keep you if you want to be kept, and keep you even if you don't have a clue as to what to do next.

Although I'm not singing as much now at age 63 as I was at age 6, I am still an advocate of good music, good lyrics, and a good performance, and to those who appreciate quality music and quality messages rest assured that, "God still wants to use YOU!!!"

CPSIA information can be obtained at www.ICGtesting.com
Printed in the USA
BVOW04s0907020914

364817BV00001B/5/P

9 781496 933447